SERVING 1

A Handbook for Children's Liturgy

Barbara Hopper writes from more than 20 years' experience of working with children's liturgy in both parish and school settings. In 1997, she completed an MA in Pastoral Studies at Heythrop College, London. She now divides her time between two part-time posts: Parish Administrator at St Thomas More, Bramley, Surrey, and Liturgy Adviser in the Diocese of Arundel and Brighton.

SERVING THE CHURCH

Series Editors: Michael and Kathleen Walsh

A Handbook
for
Children's Liturgy

Barbara Mary Hopper

CANTERBURY
PRESS

Norwich

Text and illustrations © Barbara Mary Hopper 2003

First published in 2003 by the Canterbury Press Norwich
(a publishing imprint of Hymns Ancient & Modern Limited,
a registered charity)
St Mary's Works, St Mary's Plain,
Norwich, Norfolk NR3 3BH

www.scm-canterburypress.co.uk

British Library Cataloguing in Publication data

A catalogue record for this book is available
from the British Library.

ISBN 1-85311-551-7

Typeset by Rowland Phototypesetting Ltd,
Bury St Edmunds, Suffolk
Printed and bound by
Biddles Ltd, www.biddles.co.uk

Contents

Abbreviations

AFW	*Alternative Futures for Worship*, vol. 1
CAC	*Children in the Assembly of the Church*
CL	'Constitution on the Liturgy', Vatican II
DMC	*Directory for Masses with Children*
GIF	*Growing into Faith*
Guidelines	Liturgy of the Word with Children *Guidelines*
NDSW	*The New Dictionary of Sacramental Worship*

Acknowledgements

The text of the Emmaus story – Luke 24:13–35 – is taken from the *New Jerusalem Bible*, published and copyright 1985 by Darton, Longman & Todd Ltd and Doubleday, a division of Random House Inc., and used by permission of the publishers.

All the Gospel passages quoted from the *Lectionary for Masses with Children* are scripture taken from the *Contemporary English Version*, copyright 1995 of the American Bible Society, New York, NY 10023 (www.americanbible.org), used with permission. Indeed it has given permission to copy these passages for use in children's take-home sheets.

The English translation of the *Directory for Masses with Children* from *Documents on the Liturgy, 1963–1979: Conciliar, Papal, and Curial Texts*, copyright 1982, International Committee on English in the Liturgy, Inc. All rights reserved.

Liturgy of the Word with Children *Guidelines*. A document approved by the Department for Christian Life and Worship in November 1996, copyright 1996, Bishops' Conference of England and Wales.

Series introduction

This is one of a series of handbooks designed to help lay people play a greater part in the life of the Church. It is usual nowadays to find lay men and women reading at Mass, administering Communion, organizing children's liturgy, even sometimes leading eucharistic services in the absence of a priest. Lay people commonly organize the music for Mass and other liturgical events in the parish. Many are asked to help out in other ways, sometimes even outside the boundaries of the parish, by becoming, for example, governors of the local Catholic school.

For all these tasks, and other roles that the laity now play, the authors of the books in this series have tried to describe what is entailed in the particular role or ministry to which you have been called. They have provided something of the history and the theology where appropriate. They understand that people are willing, but often need encouragement to take on tasks that, in the past, may have seemed the special preserve of the clergy.

They also understand that those approached to undertake these ministries are often busy people with jobs to do and families to care for. The books are therefore as concise as it is possible to make them, written in straightforward language with a minimum of technical jargon (though glossaries are supplied where necessary) and include a good deal of practical advice.

We hope that these books will be helpful, not just in the practical details of fulfilling a ministry within the Church, but also in developing a deeper, more spiritual understanding of the mysteries of the Catholic faith.

Kathleen and Michael Walsh

Introduction

After the family Mass one Sunday, five-year-old Thomas, together with his older sister Isabel and younger brother Dominic, came up to the priest and tugged his chasuble to gain attention. Thomas enquired, 'Father, when are we going to have Pray School again?' The priest was perplexed until their parents explained that this was the name their children used for children's liturgy of the word. Then Isabel added her own thoughts: 'Father, I really like it when we go into your house to have our own Bible story. Will it be next Sunday?'

The family's description, 'Pray School', captures the essence of what is celebrated most Sundays of the year during term time in that parish: a school of worship that has an important role in forming and building faith, a liturgy through which the children are enabled to understand the word of God and respond in prayer at their own level. How did this 'Pray School' that Thomas and Isabel were so keen to take part in come about?

I

Beginnings

While I was working as a lay missionary in Ghana in the early 1970s the task of implementing the liturgical reforms, described in the *Constitution on the Sacred Liturgy of the Second Vatican Council*, was well under way. In parts of north-east Ghana there were at that time few adult Catholics, but increasing numbers of adults, with their children, being enrolled in the Catechumenate. Once enrolled they would take part in the lengthy process of preparation for baptism. Most tribal groups did not yet have even the Gospels in their own languages. Though many were illiterate, there was still an urgent need for the Gospels, at least, to be translated for use in the liturgies.

In each language area, a priest or two, together with the help of a few catechists, took it in turns to spend the early part of each week translating the Gospel passage for the Sunday into the local language, plus one of the other readings if they had time. Then, towards the end of the week, the carefully typed pages were taken by volunteers on bicycle or on foot to all the priests and catechists throughout the language area so that they could be used during the coming Sunday's liturgy. In each outstation, if a priest was present Mass was celebrated; if not, the catechist led a liturgy of the word. In either case, afterwards, the catechumens were taken aside in various groups – men, women, young people and children – for further reflection on what they had heard, each group being led by a catechist and a helper.

Observing the unrelenting task of translation week by week, knowing that it would take many years to complete the three-year cycle, brought home to me, as never before, the importance of God's word and how vital it is to our faith development to be able to hear the word and respond to it in our own language and culture.

On my return from West Africa in 1976, I joined the small rural parish community of Our Lady of the Forest, in Forest Row, Sussex. Shortly before my arrival, the priest, Father Geoffrey Burke, had started working with a small group of parishioners to implement one of the proposals from the *Directory for Masses with Children* (given in full in Appendix 1). The particular suggestion, for use during adult Masses in which children participate, is: 'Sometimes, moreover, if the place itself and the nature of the individuals permit, it possibly will be appropriate to celebrate the liturgy of the word, including a homily, with the children in a separate, but not too distant, location. Then, before the eucharistic liturgy begins, the children are led to the place where the adults have meanwhile celebrated their own liturgy of the word' (DMC, 17). Here, at last, was a way to enable children to hear God's word and respond to it at their own level!

Father Burke, as a result of his experience as a religious education adviser for schools in the Archdiocese of Southwark, was acutely aware that most children find Mass boring. Although Mass at that time was celebrated in English, the readings were still unintelligible for younger children. Along with many other people, Father Burke and the parishioners welcomed the *Directory*'s provision of many simple but profound ways in which the Mass can speak to children and form them.

Initially the task of preparing and leading a separate liturgy of the word for children was quite daunting, for there were no guidelines other than the very brief statement quoted above. No resource books had been written, nor was there a lectionary for children with somewhat simplified versions of the Sunday scripture readings. We belonged to one of the first parishes in the country to undertake this task, so we couldn't visit other parishes to see how they tackled it. (In fact, people from other parishes gradually started coming to consult us! We were not 'experts', but we did have some ideas to share from our experience.) However, we were very fortunate that our priest was able to train and guide us. From his own background in catechetics and liturgy, he was able to give us a sure grounding in liturgical principles and under his guidance we prepared liturgies for the children. These followed the shape of the adult liturgy of the word. From the outset, Father Burke impressed on us the fact that we were engaged in celebrating a liturgy with the children, not running a crèche!

It was an awesome task for us to become the presiders for the children during their own liturgy of the word, which, at the time, was a leap forward for lay involvement in liturgy. Father Burke encouraged, guided and reassured us and helped us to plan each liturgy. It showed a real commitment on his part and was a wonderful experience of collaborative ministry for all involved. However, because he was always presiding at the Mass, he could never be present at the children's own liturgies, so he was interested to know, via our reflections and the feedback from families, how these celebrations were working out.

We formed a group, which consisted of several parents, mums and dads, a grandfather and two primary school teachers. Each person had their own experience of communicating with young children and we shared the same desire: to open the message of the scriptures to these little ones. We were committed to helping the new generation of Christians in our parish family to grow in faith and enjoy celebrating it.

Up to that time, there had been very few opportunities for lay people to receive liturgical formation. Even as a Catholic teacher, I found it difficult at first to keep in mind that what we were to offer the children was to be a liturgy – a public act of worship, not a religious education lesson. As the only books we could find at the time to help us plan our presentation of the Sunday Gospel readings and our exploration of their meanings for the children were the RE books we used at school, I needed to remind myself almost constantly of what we were about and why we had this permission to take the children aside to celebrate their own liturgy of the word.

Thinking back to those tentative beginnings, I can see now how some things could have been celebrated better, but we did try to learn from our mistakes. We were open to new insights and those of us who continue to be engaged in this ministry are still learning.

Sometimes, moreover, if the place itself and the nature of the individuals permit, it possibly will be appropriate to celebrate the liturgy of the word, including a homily, with the children in a separate, but not too distant, location. Then, before the eucharistic liturgy begins, the children are led to the place where the adults have meanwhile celebrated their own liturgy of the word.

Directory for Masses with Children, 17

Where do we start?

What ages are the children?

During the first couple of years of celebrating children's liturgy of the word at Forest Row, the children chosen to have their own separate liturgy of the word were aged five, six and seven. Although I was not there at the very start of the project, I believe the reason for choosing this age range was a concern that, coming up to and during First Communion preparation, it was particularly important that the children should not feel bored at Mass. They should be specially helped towards 'full, conscious, active participation, which the nature of the liturgy itself requires and which, in virtue of their baptism, is the right and duty of the Christian people' (CL, 14).

Initially, the children went aside for their own liturgy of the word every third or fourth Sunday in school term time. We were concerned about quality, not quantity. Gradually these celebrations became more frequent as the competence and number of the liturgy leaders and helpers increased: eventually the children had their own celebrations on about 30 Sundays of the year.

In the years that followed, three groups developed, each with their own liturgy leaders and helpers. The age ranges were four- to five-year-olds, six- to eight-year-olds and nine plus. This was because the parish had a growing number of young families and there were three preparatory schools, with children who boarded, so those who were Catholic came to our church on Sundays during term time and were catered for in the nine plus group.

The priest's house is attached to the church and so it was easy for the children to process from the church into the house. The rooms are fairly small, though, and the number of children was increasing, so it was necessary on a practical level to divide them into the three groups. However, even if larger rooms had been available, we would still have opted for three groups so that the language, images and examples used to present the Gospel message would be appropriate to the different levels of understanding and experience of the children.

In a few parishes I have seen all the children, aged from about 2 to 12, being taken into one large room or hall to celebrate a liturgy of the word all together. In this situation, it is likely that the celebration goes over the heads of the youngest and seems childish to the oldest. The risk that both these age groups become bored is very real. So, my recommendation is that grouping children into fairly narrow age ranges is the ideal arrangement.

Recruiting – who should we invite?

The best approach would seem to be to invite some parishioners who are not much involved in ministry in the parish or else not yet involved to come together to see what it is all about, without committing to anything. They could then decide whether or not they would take part as a liturgy leader or helper. Young parents, youthful grandparents, young people in the top years of secondary school and relative newcomers to the parish would be some people who could be approached and invited. Teachers and catechists could also be recruited, as long as they recognize and respond to the difference between giving an RE lesson or leading a First Communion session and celebrating children's liturgy.

Whenever I have given a talk aimed at recruiting leaders and helpers, I have always made the promise that, if you volunteer as a helper, you will not be pressured into becoming a leader. People who can play a musical instrument or lead the children in song would also add to the gifts of the group. The requirements of the Guidelines on Child Protection (which are covered in more detail in Chapter 5) need to be followed in full with regard to recruiting and carrying out the ministry of the members of the group when celebrating with the children.

Tools for planning

Where the parish is planning to introduce children's liturgy of the word or renew or reform what is happening already, some considerable discussion will be needed before a start is made. The aspects of celebrating liturgy with children are covered here, as well as practical examples and suggested resources.

The best approach is to start by reading through the Liturgy of the Word with Children *Guidelines* (reproduced in full in Appendix 2). It is vital to know the shape of liturgy, as applied to children's liturgy of the word, and Chapter 3 provides a detailed framework within which to plan each celebration. Then, in Chapter 4 there is a ten-point guide to planning, with an explanation and examples at each stage. You may also find it helpful to read through the examples of liturgies given in Chapters 6, 7 and 8. These give a 'feel' of what is being celebrated and stimulate creative thinking. Apply the steps for planning a liturgy to the Gospel of the particular Sunday, then celebrate it with the chosen age group of children, meeting later to evaluate and, if necessary, refine your strategy. If you begin by celebrating liturgy with children of one age group, about once a month, this will give ample time for planning and evaluating in between.

The following charts help you to see at a glance the parallel between the adults' celebration and that of the children. Chart 1 applies if the children go to celebrate their separate liturgy immediately after the opening song and greeting. The elements printed in **bold** are the essential elements to celebrate with the children. The other elements are optional. Chart 2 applies if the children are not called forward to go to their own liturgy room until after the opening prayer.

Chart 1

INTRODUCTORY RITES

Opening Song

Greeting

Assembly in the church	*Children in their liturgy room*
	Introducing the message
Penitential Rite	Penitential Rite
Gloria (in season)	**Gloria** (in season)

LITURGY OF THE WORD

Opening Prayer	
First Reading	
Responsorial Psalm	
Second Reading	
Gospel Acclamation	**Gospel Acclamation**
Gospel	**Gospel**
Homily	**Dialogue to explore the scriptures, and response**
Creed	Creed (simplified)
Intercessions	**Intercessions**
Collection	Collection

LITURGY OF THE EUCHARIST

Formation and training: how to go about initial training in the parish

Initially the liturgy leaders and helpers will learn by meeting together to plan, celebrate liturgies with the children and then evaluate. There

Chart 2

INTRODUCTORY RITES

Opening Song

Greeting

Penitential Rite

Gloria (in season)

Opening Prayer

LITURGY OF THE WORD

Assembly in the church	*Children in their liturgy room*
	Introducing the message
First Reading	
Responsorial Psalm	
Second Reading	
Gospel Acclamation	**Gospel Acclamation**
Gospel	**Gospel**
Homily	**Dialogue to explore the scriptures, and response**
Creed	Creed (simplified)
Intercessions	**Intercessions**
Collection	Collection

LITURGY OF THE EUCHARIST

---

may be someone in the group, or from a neighbouring parish, who has experience of celebrating the liturgy of the word with children who could be asked to advise and guide. It's when people are guided to plan a liturgy, using the tools mentioned above (and are even given the opportunity to try it out with a group of their own children beforehand, so as to gauge, through their children's response, whether or not they are using the most appropriate style of language) that people begin to find the confidence to lead. Once they have actually celebrated several liturgies and evaluated them, confidence in the use of the tools for preparation grows.

Many dioceses have someone on their diocesan liturgy commission or religious formation team who has a particular expertise in children's liturgy who can be consulted. Quite often, there are courses or presentations and training sessions at diocesan level and within deaneries or groups of parishes.

After a time exercising their ministry as liturgy leaders for children's liturgy, some of the members in our team at Forest Row felt the need to borrow books from the parish library to read more about the scripture readings. Later, six members of our group completed a Diocesan Certificate Course in order to deepen their understanding of their faith and of scripture in particular.

Presenting the idea to the parish

Once the team of leaders and helpers for children's liturgy has studied and planned together, it is very important that the idea be presented to the parish. If possible, the parish priest should do this, perhaps using a homily in which to do so or weaving the idea gently into various homilies over several weeks. A priest or deacon is permitted to preach about aspects of the celebration of Mass, not just about the readings. However, the priest may not feel able to do justice to the subject and so he could invite a lay person to speak about it at the end of Mass. It would also be very helpful to have an item in the parish newsletter or, better still, a simple leaflet to hand out to people. Having a leaflet will enable the information to be disseminated throughout the parish as people will take extra copies to give to their friends and families who do not attend Mass at your church regularly.

It is important to let all the parishioners know that the permission to take the children aside for their own liturgy of the word comes from the *Directory for Masses with Children* and is not just some idea dreamt up by the priest or the parish liturgy group! It is also helpful to explain that the children will be exploring the meaning of the Sunday Gospel, so it's not a crèche or childminding exercise; nor is it the opportunity for extra First Communion preparation or an occasion when the children can rehearse for the Christmas pageant or carol service! People need to realize that the children are going aside to celebrate a liturgy, not for a 'lesson'. It may be desirable to arrange a couple of meetings for parishioners, especially parents – one during the day and a repeat one evening – during which the idea can be presented, together with a demonstration liturgy.

The age range of the children invited to take part needs to be stated clearly. Also, it should be pointed out that the children are invited, not obliged, to join the children's liturgy group and that the parents are to remain in the church. Otherwise you are likely to find parents accompanying their children to the liturgy and bringing younger siblings with them. (An exception may be made for the first couple of liturgies that a young child attends for the first time if they are unsure or reluctant to leave their parents.) Parents should remain in the church for the 'adult' liturgy, where they can be nourished by the readings and homily at their own level.

Some people can be upset by the fact that an age range of children has been selected, especially when their own child is outside that range. However, the reasons can be set out and, if the parish is starting or restarting children's liturgy, people should appreciate that it is important to start with one group in the hope that, later on, with additional leaders and helpers and more experience, another age group can also be catered for.

Getting started

Once the idea has been presented to the parish and a realistic starting date announced, it is time to get on with the planning. The group of liturgy leaders and helpers will need to decide, with the priest, whether the children are to be called forward by the priest to go to their own liturgy room after the opening song and greeting of the

Mass (see 'A Model' in *Guidelines)* or before the first reading. Having the children gather in a parish room or hall before Mass begins is not an option, because, as pointed out in the *Guidelines* from the Bishops' Conference, 'to emphasize the unity of the whole assembly, the children gather with their families for the introductory rites of the Mass' (see the 'Commentary' section in *Guidelines*).

Once the sending out time has been decided, during that particular Sunday Mass over a series of weeks, make sure someone discretely times how many minutes the celebration of the Mass takes from that point until the end of the homily. This will give some idea as to how much time you will have with the children for their own celebration.

A separate liturgy of the word with children is an opportunity for the children to:

- hear God's word using a simpler version of the scripture from a children's lectionary
- explore the meaning of Sunday's Gospel
- be helped to make an appropriate response in prayer and action.

It is *not:*

- a crèche
- a childminding exercise
- an RE lesson
- a chance to have an extra session for First Communion preparation
- the occasion to rehearse a nativity play or practise for the carol service

It is a liturgy – an act of worship.

The times will vary slightly from week to week, according to the length of the readings and whether the psalm is sung or not. It will also depend on the length of the homily, which can vary from one preacher to another, but this should still give you a reasonable idea of how much time there is.

Having established the approximate duration of the liturgy to be celebrated, all that remains is to plan what to do and decide who will undertake the various ministries: leader, reader, helper and musician.

3

The shape of liturgy

It is essential to realize that there is a shape to liturgy. Every act of worship has, or should have, the same underlying shape. The story of the two disciples on the road to Emmaus reveals that shape and reflects the essentials of any good liturgy. Let us look afresh at this well-known resurrection narrative.

The road to Emmaus (Luke 24:13–35)

Now that very same day, two of them were on their way to a village called Emmaus, seven miles from Jerusalem, and they were talking together about all that had happened. And it happened that as they were talking together and discussing it, Jesus himself came up and walked by their side; but their eyes were prevented from recognising him. He said to them, 'What are all these things that you are discussing as you walk along?' They stopped, their faces downcast.

Then one of them, called Cleopas, answered him, 'You must be the only person staying in Jerusalem who does not know the things that have been happening there these last few days.' He asked, 'What things?' They answered, 'All about Jesus of Nazareth, who showed himself a prophet powerful in action and speech before God and the whole people; and how our chief priests and our leaders handed him over to be sentenced to death, and had him crucified. Our own hope had been that he would be the one to set Israel free. And this is not all: two whole days have now gone by since it all happened; and some women from our group have astounded us: they went to the tomb in the early morning, and when they could not find the body, they came back to tell us they had seen a vision of angels who declared he was alive. Some of our friends went to the tomb and found everything exactly as the women had reported, but of him they saw nothing.'

Then he said to them, 'You foolish men! So slow to believe all the prophets have said! Was it not necessary that the Christ should suffer before entering into his glory?' Then, starting with Moses and going through all the prophets, he explained to them the passages throughout the scriptures that were about himself.

When they drew near to the village to which they were going, he made as if to go on; but they pressed him to stay with them saying, 'It is nearly evening, and the day is almost over.' So he went in to stay with them. Now while he was with them at table, he took the bread and said the blessing; then he broke it and handed it to them. And their eyes were opened and they recognised him; but he had vanished from their sight. Then they said to each other, 'Did not our hearts burn within us as he talked to us on the road and explained the scriptures to us?'

They set out that instant and returned to Jerusalem. There they found the Eleven assembled together with their companions, who said to them, 'The Lord has indeed risen and has appeared to Simon.' Then they told their story of what had happened on the road and how they had recognized him at the breaking of bread.

How does this reveal the shape of liturgy?

Those two disciples, walking along the road to Emmaus, were talking about things that had actually happened in their lives. They were devastated by the crucifixion of Jesus and confused by the rumour that he had risen from the dead. They were on a **journey** – an actual journey between Jerusalem and Emmaus as well as an inner journey of discovery about Jesus.

When Jesus came along (though they did not know it was Jesus), he asked them what they were talking about. They shared their journey and their experiences with him. There was a **meeting** of three people: a meeting of minds and hearts, not just a meeting of convenience to share a long walk.

Then Jesus explained the scriptures to them. The **word** of God was used by Jesus to shed light on their recent experiences.

The disciples' hearts had burned within them as Jesus had opened up the meaning of the scriptures to them. They recognized Jesus in the breaking of bread. Both these things show that the disciples made a heartfelt **response** to Jesus' presence.

Then the two disciples did something that was most unwise in normal circumstances: they set out immediately and returned to Jerusalem to tell their story to the other disciples. They risked the dangers of travelling by night (robbers and wild animals) because they were aglow with a sense of **mission**.

So, this story of the disciples on the road to Emmaus reflects the essentials of any good liturgy. In the liturgy, you are always on safe ground if you follow this pattern:

- journey
- meeting
- word
- response
- mission

Like those disciples, whatever we are celebrating in the liturgy, it must be real. Liturgy, such as Sunday Mass, is not supposed to be something set apart from life. We come to celebrate the struggles of life and faith, the struggle to come close to God. Liturgy is the celebration of our real lives, in union with God, a part of our journey through life. In fact, liturgy should be at the centre of our living, reflecting and celebrating.

As Christians, we do not journey alone. We are called to come together as the Body of Christ, the Church. This coming together is intended to be more than being a crowd. We express in our gathering together our shared faith, hopes and desire to love and be loved and support one another.

In the varied experiences of life, God's word in the scriptures makes sense of it all. On our journey, like the disciples on the road to Emmaus, we meet Jesus and one another. We listen to and reflect on the word of God, allowing it to illuminate and clarify our experiences.

We respond with words and gestures in a very concrete way that indicates either a change in direction or a coming back to the path or a continuation of the journey with renewed conviction and energy. At Mass, we respond by 'giving thanks' and accepting the Lord's invitation to 'take and eat'.

In all of this, like the disciples, we do not want simply to keep it all to ourselves, but, rather, we want to talk about these experiences. Our desire is to serve the Lord and witness that he has done marvels for us. Good liturgy should lead us to go out with renewed enthusiasm to love and serve the Lord.

To put it even more simply, the pattern of good liturgy, celebrated within the journey of life, is to:

- gather
- listen
- respond
- go

This pattern guides the shape of all celebrations of children's liturgy as well as being the shape of the whole of Mass.

The shape of children's liturgy of the word

Let us apply this shape to the liturgy of the word with children so we can put everything into the correct order.

Gather

- The children gather with their families in the church for the introductory rite of the Mass. (It may be helpful to have laminated cards with the word 'RESERVED' on them to put on the seats of the children, their leaders and helpers while they are away in their own liturgy room.)

- After the opening song and greeting, the children, their leaders and helpers are called forward by the presider (the alternative is to do this after the opening prayer).

- A copy of a children's lectionary is presented to one of the children, the leader or a helper with these or similar words: 'My dear children, you will now go to hear God's word, to praise God in song and to reflect on the wonderful things God has done for us. We will await your return so that, together, we may celebrate the Eucharist.'

- The children, their leaders and helpers then process to their nearby liturgy room, perhaps led by an altar server.

- They enter the room quietly. An ideal room has a carpet or carpet squares for the children to sit on, a low table with a coloured cloth (the colour of the liturgical season, perhaps), a lighted candle, crucifix and other appropriate visual aids. The table is not called an 'altar' – that is in the church.

- When the children have gathered in the room, the leader introduces the particular message that is to be the focus of their celebration.

- A simple penitential rite and/or gloria are used (unless the children have already celebrated this in the church with the whole assembly and did not leave until after the opening prayer).

Listen

- The leader sets the scene for proclaiming the Gospel, using ideas from the children's own experience.

- Before the Gospel is read by the reader, everyone stands for the sung acclamation.

- The scripture (usually the Gospel) is proclaimed by a leader or helper, using a version and style of reading appropriate to the level of understanding of the children in the group.

- The leader then opens up the meaning of the scripture for the children by establishing a dialogue. The leader's task is to form a 'bridge' from life experience to scripture and back.

- The scripture passage is explored with the aid of discussion, reflection and other appropriate activities, such as the use of visual aids and mime.

Respond

- One response could be to lead the children in a simple litany of praise specially devised to correspond to the theme drawn from the scripture reading.

- Another possibility might be to use a psalm as a response after the Gospel.

- There could be a discussion with the children to help them decide and agree to do something to respond to the message, either during the rest of the Mass or at home or school later in the week.

- When the altar server or person responsible for giving the signal that the homily has ended in the church arrives, the leader needs to summarize very briefly the message and the response.

- The children could then be led in a simple creed.

- Intercessions should then be led and may be added to by the children as appropriate.

Go

- The children are led from their liturgy room by the leader and, perhaps, an altar server; then they process quietly back into the church to take part in the procession of the gifts.

- Ideally, part of the response discussed with the children should include something to look out for, listen for or take part in very consciously during the Liturgy of the Eucharist.

- A part of the response should be the encouragement to tell the family after Mass about the scripture story and what the children did in the group, as well as talking about the little task that everyone agreed they would try to do during the coming week.

- The children could also be encouraged to tell a friend about what they heard and did in their liturgy group. You are never too young to share the Good News!

- It may be helpful to devise a special worksheet to be given to all the children as they leave after Mass. This could include the text of the Gospel, the message which was the focus of the children's celebration, together with a picture or activity that the children could do with the help of their families. In preparing such handouts, it is most important that copyright is not infringed. (On one of the front pages of a resource book with worksheets or a book of clip art, you will find that the uses for which permission is given to photocopy parts of the book such that copyright is not being infringed are clearly stated, together with whatever restrictions apply.) It may also be desirable to acknowledge the source of the material that appears on any worksheet you produce.

- A note could also be included in the parish newsletter about what the children's liturgy has focused on, together with a suggestion for responding to that message in the family.

All this may sound rather technical, but, in the following chapters, I will give a detailed plan for preparing a liturgy, followed by three sample liturgies. These show clearly the way in which the shape – gather, listen, respond, go – is fleshed out in order to become a real celebration of God's word for the children.

The pattern of good liturgy,
celebrated within the journey of life, is to:
gather   listen   respond   go

4

Planning a liturgy of the word for children

Preparation and planning are essential to good liturgy, and forward planning for a season, such as Eastertide, enables the children's liturgy group to identify which Sundays and festivals it would be more appropriate for the whole assembly to celebrate together and which separately. The great feasts of the Church's year – Christmas, Easter and so on – are times for adults and children to be together (see the 'Preparation' section of *Guidelines*, Appendix 2).

The process of planning a liturgy

As soon as you have decided the date of the celebration, you will need, first of all, to refer to the 'Diocesan Ordo', which can be found in the *Diocesan Directory*, to check which Sunday or Solemnity is being celebrated on that date. This includes finding out whether it is Year A, B or C. (The year changes on the liturgical calendar on the First Sunday of Advent each year.) Also it can happen that a Holy Day or Solemnity, such as the Feast of the Presentation of the Lord, the Feast of Saints Peter and Paul or the Feast of the Dedication of the Cathedral may take place on the Sunday, so it is vital to check this right at the start.

Once you know which Sunday of the year or Solemnity is being celebrated, look up the readings for that occasion in a missal or the lectionary. Even though you will not be using that version of the readings with the children, it is very important to let the word of God for that day speak to your heart so that you find a message for yourself from those readings, especially from the Gospel. Clearly preparation needs to begin early so that you have time to reflect on it prayerfully. (For a very straightforward and readable commentary on the Gospels, see the appropriate volume of William Barclay's *The Daily Study Bible*, published by The Saint Andrew Press.) It is important for liturgy leaders, musicians and helpers to plan together, each reflecting on God's word before, and after, the group meets.

The Bishops' Conference of the United States has produced a *Lectionary for Masses with Children*. In the absence of such a lectionary approved by the Bishops' Conference for England and Wales, this provides a child-friendly translation, though other translations are available. There is a power in the word of God, so, when they were preparing the lectionary mentioned above, the authors sought to translate the text into simpler English for children, but not move so far from the original as to lose the dignity of the text. There is a temptation to go to any children's Bible to look for the story that corresponds to the Gospel passage in the adult lectionary, but such versions are at best paraphrases and often the author is retelling the story in their own words. It is acceptable to edit the scripture passage from the children's lectionary slightly for your proclamation of it to the children, but not to rewrite it in your own words (DMC, 43). Following the reading, it is often a good idea to retell the story to the children in the dialogue that follows. For this, other versions of the text from a children's Bible or a resource book may be useful.

It is important that the actual book the priest presents to the children and their liturgy leaders and helpers when he calls them forward to process to their own liturgy room – the book from which the Gospel will be read to the children – should be suitably worthy. It should, preferably, be hardback and of a good size, a book that shows the importance of God's word, and always handled and carried with reverence and care.

From everyone's personal reflection on the message of God's word for that Sunday, the group should decide on a one-line message or good news item to focus on during the celebration with the children – a succinct message that could be written on a piece of paper as small as a business card. This is good advice for preachers also, for if they cannot tell you the message in a similarly succinct way, there probably isn't one.

If you consider the Gospel story for the Second Sunday in Ordinary Time, Year C – the account of Jesus changing water into wine at the marriage feast at Cana – there are several messages that could be chosen. For example:

- Jesus showed a sign of his power and his disciples believed in him
- Jesus' love will never run out
- Jesus brings happiness to people who trust in him
- Jesus' word has the power to change us
- Jesus can transform our lives if we truly offer ourselves to him.

The last two messages would be appropriate for teenagers and adults. In choosing the message, the age, understanding and experience of the children need to be kept in mind. Also, recall what message was chosen when the same Gospel story was celebrated with that group previously.

Once agreed on, the message should be easily recognized, woven into the script of the liturgy.

Keep in mind the shape of the liturgy – gather, listen, respond, go – and refer to the elements that come into each section. When planning with a group, it can be helpful to write those four headings on the sheet as a reminder of the shape and order the liturgy should follow. Although the heading 'gather' comes first, the central element of the liturgy is the reading of the Gospel and the dialogue to discover its message, so the 'listen' part should be planned first.

Now, look up the ideas given for the celebration you are planning in whatever resource books you have available. It is good to have a variety of resource books and there is a list at the end of the book. Some are written with young children in mind, while others present ideas for varying age ranges of children. With the group, look at all the ideas you have gathered together, then, keeping your chosen message in view, simply bounce ideas off one another. Often the group comes up with an idea, approach or development that was not presented in any of the books.

More than once I have noticed liturgy leaders on Sunday morning taking their only resource book from the shelf, plus a book of photocopyable pictures or worksheets, rushing to the photocopier, making copies for the children to colour in during their liturgy, picking up a box of colouring pencils, a candle and a box of matches and putting them in the liturgy room just before Mass begins. In such a situation, the liturgy leader would seem to have reflected too little on the Gospel for that Sunday. Furthermore, using the resource book alone, slavishly, cannot possibly supply all that's needed. There is no substitute for proper planning and the prayerful reflection of the liturgy leader.

Good practice means that the group first needs to think of ideas as to how to build a bridge from the children's everyday lives towards the Gospel reading for the day. It may be that a character in the Gospel story is unfamiliar, as, for example, in the Gospel for the 29th Sunday, Year C – the parable of the widow and the judge (Luke 18:1–8). Faced with this reading, one group of liturgy leaders and helpers came together to plan their liturgy for a group of young children and they asked themselves if all the children would know who a widow is or what a judge does and decided that some of the young children would probably not know. So, they devised a dramatized version to present to the children after the Gospel reading. One leader was the judge and put on a graduate gown and a wig, a second leader was the widow and put on a shawl and headscarf and the reader was the narrator. This dramatization, together with the knocking and pleading gestures of the widow, was most effective.

Various visual aids may be needed, so you should decide who is going to prepare them and assemble the display, if necessary. Then, choose a suitable Gospel acclamation – preferably one that can be sung.

Sometimes it may be appropriate for some of the helpers and children to use percussion instruments – shakers and tambourines, for example – to accompany the Gospel acclamation. (Remember, however, not to use 'Alleluia' in the Gospel acclamation during Lent.)

Gospel acclamations

- 'Alleluia, Listen to Jesus' by Bernadette Farrell, *Share the Light*.
- 'Alleluia, We Will Listen' and
- 'Feed Us With Your Word', both by Paul Inwood, *Children at Heart*.
- 'Listen, His Words Are For You' by Christopher Walker, *Music for Children's Liturgy of the Word – Cycle A*.
- 'Praise to you, O Christ our Saviour' by Bernadette Farrell, *Laudate*, 200.

Next, you need to work out how to develop the dialogue to draw the message out with the children. This will give you the essentials of the 'Listen' section.

The next step is to consider an appropriate response. This can be an activity, song, prayer, litany or other liturgical action whereby the children can respond to the message of the Gospel reading. Decide how to lead the children to respond and list what you may need to prepare in advance – candles, holy water, the song and gestures, prayer, litany and so on. Practice in responding to the word varies widely, but leaders who engage children in drawing, colouring and poster-making on a regular basis as the primary or sole form of response to the word, though undoubtedly well intentioned, do the children a disservice. In fact, the *Guidelines* warn against replacing reflection on the Gospel 'with activity alone, lest others perceive this gathering as a containment exercise or Sunday school rather than an act of worship' (see the 'Responding to the Word' section in the *Guidelines*).

If your group is starting a separate liturgy of the word for children for the first time in the parish, it is worthwhile giving some thought to how you will transfer the children from their families into the liturgy room. The priest will need to be involved as he has to call the

---

Suggestions for music

Penitential rite
- 'Kyrie' from *Jubilee Mass* by Owen Alstott.
- 'God of Mercy' (*with signing*) by Bernadette Farrell, *Share the Light*.

Gloria
- 'Gloria' (*with hand claps*) by Mike Anderson, *Laudate*, 530.
- 'Gloria' by Anne Ward, *Laudate*, 525.
- 'Gloria!' by George Salazar with music arranged by Stephen Dean, *Laudate*, 532.
- 'Glory to God' from the Mass for the Journey by Mark Friedman and Janet Vogt, *Enter the Journey*.
- 'Sing to God a song of glory' by Francesca Leftley, *Hymns Old and New*, 491.

---

children, their leaders and helpers forward and present them with their lectionary. Also, if you would like the children to be led in procession from the church to their liturgy room (and back again at the end), you will need to liaise with the altar servers. There may also be other practical issues, such as obtaining the necessary keys to unlock the liturgy room.

Having worked out the mechanics of getting into the liturgy room and with the essentials of the 'listen' and 'respond' sections in mind, the group then needs to formulate how to 'gather' the children. This involves deciding on the words that will be used to introduce the message – the good news that is to be the focus of the celebration, perhaps a penitential rite, and a gloria (except during Advent and Lent).

If the children are too young to read a hymnbook for a version of the gloria, they could simply join in the chorus or refrain with song and gesture, perhaps, while a cantor sings the verses. The important thing is to lead the children in praising God.

Give some thought to something you could encourage the children to look out for or pray for during the rest of the Mass (preferably related to the message they have been focusing on). Work into your plan what you will encourage the children to tell the family afterwards and the response that they might make at home or school during the coming week.

Decide who is going to come to give you the signal that the homily has just ended in the Church.

If a simplified creed is desirable for the children, perhaps in an older group, compose it (see *Gather the Children* by Mary Catherine Berglund for examples). You will certainly need to compose a few suitable intercessions for the conclusion of your liturgy. There are suggestions for writing these in the 'Commentary' section of the *Guidelines* (see Appendix 2) and it is helpful if the group follows the correct format, so that the children become accustomed to good liturgical practice from an early age.

You may decide to prepare a handout or worksheet (using material that can be photocopied without infringing copyright) to give to all the children as they leave the church at the end of Mass. These points will give you the elements you need for the 'go' section, just before you and the children return to the church to take part in the procession of gifts and rejoin their families. Remember that, in the Mass, the liturgy of the word is not an end in itself, but leads into the liturgy of the Eucharist.

Finally, look at your liturgy plan as a whole and ask yourself the following questions.

- Is there a good balance between prayer and singing, listening and responding?
- Is there a place for silence?
- Are there changes of focus, to retain the children's attention and interest?
- Have you got an idea as to what else you could do if you have more time than you expect?

- Is there a way to shorten it, if you are called sooner than you expect, without losing the essentials of good liturgy?
- Make a checklist of who prepares what in advance – visual aids, music, setting up the room, lighting the candle, liaising with the priest, altar servers and the organizer of the procession of gifts.
- If a brief note is needed for the newsletter, to tell the parents what message the children will be reflecting on in their separate liturgy, decide who will compose it and ensure that it appears in the parish newsletter on the correct weekend.

Having planned to the best of your ability, pray through the message during the week and try to enjoy working together to open the scriptures with the children and lead them to respond in prayer. Use the examples of liturgies given in Chapters 6, 7 and 8 for ideas and getting a feel for what is possible as they have actually been celebrated. Do not worry if things do not go exactly to plan – the perfect liturgy can only be celebrated in heaven!

Summary for planning a separate liturgy of the word for children

1 The organizer finds out which Sunday of the year, Solemnity or Feast Day is to be celebrated.

2 The children's liturgy group members reflect individually on the readings in the adult lectionary for that Sunday to find what message the readings hold for them.

3 That Sunday's Gospel is then found in a children's lectionary and the group decides if it needs to be edited.

4 A one-line message or good news point to focus on during the celebration is agreed by the group.

5 The shape of liturgy – gather, listen, respond, go – is kept in view.

6 All the elements of the 'listen' section are planned.

7 The most appropriate way to 'respond' is then decided.

8 All the aspects of how the children will 'gather' are agreed.

9 All that is needed for the 'go' section is decided.

10 The liturgy plan is reviewed and checked for its balance between prayer, singing, silence, listening and responding. The group members pray and complete all the practical preparations.

Remember, the perfect liturgy can only be celebrated in heaven!

5

Ministers of the word

What qualifications are needed?

In Chapter 2 I outlined some thoughts on recruiting. People of varying ages and backgrounds are needed; people of faith who are, or are willing to become, rooted in prayer and scripture. All the people who are going to share in preparing and celebrating children's liturgy need to be willing and able to work together in a team, share their gifts and value the particular gifts of others and, above all, share their faith and understanding of God's word and his love for everyone with the children of the parish. It is important to have several liturgy leaders, readers, helpers and musicians in the group so that a rota can be drawn up using just a few of these ministers each weekend. Then, each person will have some weekends when they are celebrating the separate liturgy of the word with the children and others when they remain in the assembly. If your group is too small to do this, then maybe a separate children's liturgy of the word should only be celebrated once or twice a month.

Ministries

The ministries of leader, reader, musician and priest celebrant are described in detail in the 'Ministries' section of Liturgy of the Word with Children *Guidelines* (see Appendix 2). Often when I am working with a children's liturgy group to help train new recruits, evaluate their ministry or start or reintroduce such liturgies in the parish, I invite the group members to take part in an exercise in twos or threes. They are asked to complete the following sentences:

- 'A liturgy leader always . . .'
- 'A liturgy leader never . . .'
- 'A liturgy leader enables each person to . . .'

Although it would seem that only one of the first two sentences is needed, often using both of them throws up additional responses. When the group pools the responses to all the sentences, a profile of the approach and attitudes a liturgy leader needs emerges, as well as the practical elements involved in that role. Try this exercise with your group, and not just for the role of liturgy leader but also for the ministries of reader, musician, helper and priest celebrant. The answers that are given are sure to be pertinent to your particular situation. For example, you may decide that the role of one of the helpers is to assist a particular child who has special needs.

The liturgy leader

The leader needs to have a welcoming manner, a relaxed and affirming way of talking to children, as well as the ability to create and retain the prayerful atmosphere of the celebration.

The leader is the person who presides over the celebration, welcomes the children, leads the reflection on the scriptures and facilitates the smooth running of the liturgy. The leader may also proclaim the Gospel passage for the day, but that is more properly the role of the reader.

The reader

This role focuses on proclaiming God's word to the group audibly, clearly and reverently, with faith and understanding.

The musician

The musician leads the children in song, enabling them to pray through it. This role may also involve giving a vocal lead or playing an instrument or both.

The musician should also encourage any children who are able musicians to share in this ministry.

The priest celebrant

The priest celebrant presides over the entire liturgy of the Mass.

It is his role to acknowledge the children as members of the assembly in the introduction and invite them and their leaders and helpers to assemble and go to their own liturgy. It is also helpful if the priest celebrant speaks briefly to the children during the Liturgy of the Eucharist – perhaps before the eucharistic prayer and during the concluding rite. It is less appropriate for the priest celebrant to engage in a dialogue with the children on their return to the assembly. If this happens, there is a danger that it can become like a mini-homily. The liturgy leader has been entrusted with this role for the children during their liturgy of the word and the best time for the children to talk about their celebration is when they tell their families after Mass.

Helpers

This group is not specifically mentioned in the *Guidelines*, but this ministry is very valuable. One or more helpers can assist the leader in presenting a part of the liturgy, if they feel comfortable doing so and if it is desirable. They may gather together or create the visual aids and their role could be to assemble these beforehand and show each item to the children at the appropriate time. They can also be there as the extra adult or adults to fulfil the requirements of child protection legislation and good practice.

Caring for the children

The safety and wellbeing of the children is paramount. It is vital that everyone recruited to this ministry follows the diocesan guidelines for the protection of children and young people (this would include any teenagers under 18 years of age working in your team).

Each person needs to fill in the appropriate documents and undergo whatever checks are required before taking up their ministry in the group. Also, they need to be trained in the details of best practice in child protection. Your parochial and diocesan child protection officers should be consulted for advice, guidance and help with training, as necessary.

Good working practice

- Treat all children and young people with dignity and respect.
- Have both male and female leaders, helpers, readers and musicians in your team. Ideally, ensure that at least one man and one woman are part of leading and assisting every liturgy of the word with children.
- Plan the celebration in such a way that there are always at least two adults present.
- Physical contact should always reflect the child's or young person's needs, not the minister's needs. It should be age appropriate and generally initiated by the child rather than the adult.
- Challenge unacceptable behaviour and report all allegations and/or suspicions of abuse.
- Be good role models for children and young people to follow.

Ministries

- The liturgy leader presides over the celebration, welcomes the children, leads the reflection on the scriptures and facilitates the smooth running of the liturgy of the word for children.
- The reader proclaims God's word audibly, clearly and reverently, with faith and understanding.
- The musician gives a vocal lead and may also play an instrument to enable the children to pray in song.
- The priest celebrant presides over the entire liturgy of the Mass. His role is to acknowledge the children as members of the assembly in the introduction and to send the children and their leaders and helpers to their own liturgy of the word.
- The helper may assist the leader in presenting a part of the liturgy, create or gather the visual aids, show each item to the children at the appropriate time or simply be there as an extra adult to fulfil the requirements of child protection legislation and good practice.

6

A liturgy during Lent

A liturgy leader, reader, musician and helper prepared and celebrated this separate children's liturgy of the word for the Fourth Sunday of Lent, Year A.

They chose as the focus: 'We thank God for the gift of sight.'

The liturgy was devised for children aged four to seven. The four members of the children's liturgy group prepared the resources in advance and set up the liturgy room in good time before the Mass.

All of the children in the group had good sight, but it should be

---

Resources

- A low table covered with a purple cloth, with a crucifix in a stand and a lighted candle on it.
- Three scarves that are to be used to blindfold the children.
- A covered box of items that the children can identify by feeling, hearing or smelling, such as fruits, a wooden spoon, a plastic mug, brush, comb, sponge, a picture book; a shaker, small bell, bunch of keys; a bar of soap, some 'smell pots', each containing an item with a distinctive smell, such as crushed lemon, sliced onion, perfumed handkerchief.
- A gift-wrapped box.
- Some pictures taken from old calendars of scenery, people and animals (to be kept out of sight until needed).

possible to celebrate a similar liturgy with a group that includes children who are blind or partially sighted. Sight is a gift, but we don't all have it. This doesn't mean that God loves us less. Those of us who are blind or partially sighted have other gifts, other ways of 'seeing'. As always, adjustments will need to be made to the basic liturgy to adapt it sensitively to the particular circumstances and needs of the group.

The musician set up her guitar, music stand and music books in the liturgy room. In the church, the children's lectionary and the wording for the priest to use to call the children forward and send them to their liturgy room were put ready on the credence table for the chief server to give to the priest after the introductory rites.

One of the welcomers was reminded that the children would be returning to help carry up the offertory gifts.

One of the altar servers was briefed to lead the children's procession to their liturgy room and to return when the homily ended in the church to let the liturgy leaders know and then wait to lead the children back into the church once the song for the preparation of the gifts started.

Gather

- The liturgy team and their families sat in seats near the front, with 'reserved' labels to save their places while they were in the separate liturgy room.

- As the children arrived at the church, they sat in the pews with their families.

- The priest invited the liturgy leaders and the children forward after he had greeted the assembly.

- The children's lectionary was presented to one of the children using the wording suggested in the Guidelines (see the 'Commentary' section) and the children and their leaders formed a procession and followed the altar server into their liturgy room, which was attached to the church.

- Once there, the children sat on the carpet in silence and the children's lectionary was placed reverently on the table.

Leader: Let's put our special book of God's word on the table. Please sit down quietly on the floor.
(The liturgy leader, reader, helper and musician sat on chairs and three extra chairs were ready for the children to sit on when they were blindfolded.)

Leader: What have we come here to do?
(The leader encouraged the children to put their hands up if they wanted to answer. He encouraged the children's responses, then summarized as follows.)
We have come here so that we can listen to God's word and be helped to understand God's message more easily. Are there some things here (gesturing towards the table) that are the same as in the church? (The Bible, table, cross and candle.) Today we are going to praise and thank God for all the beautiful things that we can see.

My brothers and sisters in God's family, let us be silent for a moment and think about the times when we have failed to thank God for all the beautiful things he has made in the world. (A few moments of silence.)
    Lord Jesus, you came so that we could see the truth.

Musician (sings): Lord, have mercy.

Everyone (sings): Lord, have mercy

Leader: Lord Jesus, you bring light to those in darkness.

Musician (sings): Christ, have mercy.

Everyone (sings): Christ, have mercy.

Leader: Lord Jesus, you came to heal us and strengthen us.

Musician (sings): Lord, have mercy.

Everyone (sings): Lord, have mercy.

Leader: May almighty God have mercy on us, forgive us our sins and bring us to everlasting life.

All: Amen

Listen

Leader: I would like you all to close your eyes tightly. What can you see? Can you see a colour? Please open your eyes again. Today I would like us to think about what it would be like if we were blind.
(The leader then asked for a volunteer to sit on a chair and be blindfolded. Everyone was promised a turn and asked to stay silent, so that the children with the blindfolds on could answer for themselves. The helper assisted in putting on the blindfolds and, to keep things running smoothly, the reader and musician also helped, so that three children were seated at one time ready to tell by feel, sound or smell what it was that they had been given to identify. Occasionally the leader asked, 'What colour is it?' A child correctly said, 'Yellow' for a banana, but mostly they could only guess a colour.)

Leader: So, what is it like if you cannot see? You can feel, hear and smell and that helps you to know what things are, but you cannot know the colour. Today's Gospel is about a man who was born blind – a man who had never been able to see anything. Let us stand up to welcome the Gospel.
(The musician played the guitar and led the singing of 'Jesus, we're listening (x 3), speak to us, Lord' to the tune of 'Sing Alleluia', *Hymns Old and New*, 479.)

Leader: Please sit down, and let's all listen very carefully as N. reads the Gospel story.

Reader: (Stood to proclaim the Gospel from the children's lectionary, John 9:1, 6–12, 35–8.) A reading from the holy Gospel according to John.

One day as Jesus walked along, he saw a man who had been blind since birth. Jesus spat on the ground. He made some mud and smeared it on the man's eyes. Then he said, 'Go and wash off the mud in Siloam Pool.' The man went and washed in Siloam, which means 'One Who Is Sent'. When he had washed off the mud, he could see.

The man's neighbours and the people who had seen him begging wondered if he really could be the same man. Some of them said he was the same beggar, while others said he only looked like him. But he told them, 'I am that man.'

'Then how can you see?' they asked.

He answered, 'Someone named Jesus made some mud and smeared it on my eyes. He told me to go and wash it off in Siloam Pool. When I did, I could see.'

'Where is he now?' they asked. 'I don't know', he answered.

When Jesus heard what had happened, he went and found the man. Then Jesus asked, 'Do you have faith in the Son of Man?'

He replied, 'Sir, if you will tell me who he is, I will put my faith in him.'

'You have already seen him,' Jesus answered, 'and right now he is talking with you.' The man said, 'Lord, I put my faith in you!' Then he worshipped Jesus.

This is the Gospel of the Lord.

Leader: (He asked the following questions and elicited responses from the children.) How do you think the blind man felt about not being able to see? How did he find his way around? Why did he have to become a beggar? What did Jesus do to make the blind man see? (He explained that, in those days, saliva (spit) was thought to be like an ointment that was able to make people better.)

What do you think the blind man felt like when he opened his eyes after washing them and found that he could see? Why did Jesus heal the blind man? What did it show that Jesus thought about him? Jesus felt sorry for him, he loved him. At first the blind man didn't know who had healed him, but then he found out that it was Jesus.

What do you think he said to Jesus when he found out that he was the one who had healed him? He wanted to thank Jesus and he came to believe that Jesus was the Son of God and he worshipped him.

Jesus touched the man's eyes and his heart with the light of his love, so that the man could see who Jesus really is.

Respond

Leader: (He then showed the children the gift-wrapped box.) If someone gives you a present, what do you want to do with it? Yes, we want to open it and use it. What do you say to the person who gave it to you?

Who gave us our eyes and the gift of being able to see? God gave us the gift of sight, so what should we say to him? We want to thank God that we can see and we want to use the wonderful gift of sight. (The helper, reader and musician gave out the pictures of scenery, people and animals, one to each child.)

I would like each of you in turn to hold up your picture and tell everyone what you can see. (After the children had done this, the leader continued as follows.) Shall we now thank God in song for all the beautiful things in the world that we can see? (The musician asked the children to stand up, not too close together, and played the guitar, leading the children in the song 'The Wonders I See' from *Share the Light* by Bernadette Farrell, while the helper led the actions, so that the children could copy. Afterwards, the children sat down.)

Leader: During this week, shall we try to thank God every day for all the lovely things we can see? Maybe if we see a rainbow, a beautiful sunset, a brightly coloured picture, we can just stop and pray, 'Thank you, God.' Perhaps we can pray about it when we say our prayers at bedtime? Shall we all try to do that? Also, when we go back into the church in a few minutes, we can look out for the colours in the candle flames, the priest's vestments and the stained-glass windows. We can also look at the love in the faces of our family and friends and thank God for it.

Please remember to tell your family about our Bible story after Mass and you might like to do the blindfold game with your family as well.

Go

Leader: (He briefly recapped the message then said the following.) Let's stand and pray our special intercessions, just like the grown-ups are doing now in the church.

God gave us the gift of sight and he wants us to use all his gifts well. Jesus has told us to ask God for what we need, so as God's children we pray.

We pray that we will always thank God for the gifts he has given us. Lord hear us.

Response: Lord, graciously hear us.

Leader: We pray for people who are blind or who cannot see well and for those who care for them. Lord hear us.

Response: Lord, graciously hear us.

Leader: We pray for Doctor Richard, who does operations at Magbesseneh Clinic to help blind people see. Lord hear us.

Response: Lord, graciously hear us.

Leader: Loving Father, we ask you to listen to our prayers and give us what we need, through Jesus Christ, our Lord.

Response: Amen

Leader: We are now going to go back into church to join our families. During Mass, look out for all the beautiful things, all the lovely colours you can see and thank God for them. (Before leaving the room, the helper extinguished the candle. The altar server led the procession down the side aisle, to the back. Some of the children carried the gifts as they all processed up the centre aisle and then back to their families.)

Commentary

A priest and I used these liturgy ideas to set the scene and dialogue with the children during a children's Mass at Lourdes. They were part of a pilgrimage group of children with a variety of disabilities (except blindness) and special needs and it worked very well. Each child, with their helper, was able to participate and, as the Mass was celebrated in a meadow near a mountain stream, examples of the wonders of creation were all round us.

Setting the scene using the blindfold game is an unusually long lead into listening to the Gospel, but the effect is much more dramatic if the children can first have a brief experience of 'blindness' and then hear how Jesus enabled a blind man to see. The children obviously need to be able to respect the silence and good order of the group otherwise, if they were to shout out the answer before the blindfolded child could respond, it would spoil things for everyone.

The children could be encouraged to play the 'blindfold' game at home with their families. Some of the children will do this anyway, as part of telling their family about their liturgy.

The inclusion of Doctor Richard's work at Magbesseneh Clinic in West Africa – a project that the parish supported – was important because the children had been helping in their own small ways to raise money for it, particularly during Lent.

The language of the penitential rite may not have been fully understood by the youngest children in the group, but they would at least recognize the format from their experience of Mass. On another occasion, the children may be led more gently into a penitential rite, according to the focus chosen for the celebration.

7

A liturgy for Easter Time

This liturgy of the word was prepared by a liturgy leader, a reader, a trainee liturgy leader (who was to be a helper on this occasion) and myself in the role of musician. It was celebrated on the Sixth Sunday of Easter, Year A.

Resources for this liturgy

- A low table covered with a white or gold cloth and a crucifix in a stand.
- A lighted candle, with a paschal candle motif on it if possible, surrounded by a posy of flowers.
- A baptism candle.
- A display board with pictures (from old calendars, perhaps) of a sunrise, sunset, flames, a camp fire, sailing boats, kites, a windmill, wind turbines and trees and people experiencing the effects of a strong wind.
- Alternatively, a slide projector set ready to project slides of the above pictures on to a plain wall or low screen.
- Posters of the teaching and healing aspects of Jesus' mission.
- A large piece of firm mounting card with the caption 'Come Holy Spirit' and a supply of 'flame' cut-outs (these being the outlines of children's hands), some glue sticks or glue pens for the adults to stick the flames on to the card.

We chose as the message 'Jesus gives us his Spirit to help us to live in love.'

The liturgy was devised for children aged four to seven. The four organizers shared in preparing the resources in advance and set up the liturgy room in good time before the Mass.

See page 38 for advice on how to prepare the liturgy room on the morning of the liturgy.

Gather

See page 38 for details of arrangements before the children have made their way to the liturgy room.

Leader: Let's put our special book of God's word on the table. Please sit down quietly on the floor.

What have we come here to do? (The leader encouraged the children to put their hands up if they wanted to answer. He encouraged the children's responses, then summarized as follows.)

We have come here so that we can listen to God's word and be helped to understand God's message more easily. Are there some things here (gesturing towards the table) that are the same as in the church? (The Bible, table, cross, candle and flowers.) Is there anything special about our candle? Our candle is like the large paschal candle in the church. That candle was first lit at Easter, to show us that after Jesus rose from the dead, he wanted to share his life and the light of his love with his friends.

Today we are going to praise and thank God that Jesus gives us his Spirit to help us to live in love. Together we will pray for the help we need to love Jesus and follow his ways, so that the Spirit will be with us. Let us sing and praise God for making us and all the wonderful things in the world. (Everyone stood up and the musician played and led one of the suggested versions of the gloria on page 28).

Listen

Leader: Have you ever had to say goodbye to someone, knowing that you would not see them again for quite a long time? How did you feel about it?

Today's Gospel is about the time when Jesus was going to say goodbye to his friends and return to his Father in heaven.

Let us stand up to welcome the Gospel. (I played the guitar and led the singing of 'Listen to Jesus'.)

Leader: Please sit down, and let's all listen very carefully as N. reads the Gospel story.

Reader: (Stood to proclaim the Gospel from the children's lectionary, John 14:15–21.) A reading from the holy Gospel according to John.

Jesus said to his disciples, 'If you love me, you will do as I command. Then I will ask the Father to send you the Holy Spirit who will help you and always be with you. The Spirit will show you what is true.

'The people of this world cannot accept the Spirit, because they don't see or know him. But you know the Spirit, who is with you and will keep on living in you.

'I won't leave you like orphans. I will come back to you. In a little while the people of this world won't be able to see me, but you will see me. And because I live, you will live. Then you will know that I am one with the Father. You will know that you are one with me, and I am one with you.

'If you love me, you will do what I have said, and my Father will love you. I will also love you and show you what I am like.'

This is the Gospel of the Lord.

Leader: (The leader asked the following questions and elicited responses from the children.) Who did Jesus promise to send?

He promised to send the Holy Spirit to be a special helper to his friends. Jesus reminded his friends that we cannot see the Spirit, but we can know that the Spirit is with us.

The Holy Spirit is invisible. One of the ways of thinking about the Spirit is to think about the wind. Another way is to think about light.

(The leader then guided the children through a discussion of the pictures on the display board or the sequence of slides, looking first at how we can experience the presence and power of the wind. It can move things in a particular direction, such as tree branches, autumn leaves and kites; it can be strong and very helpful, as with sailing boats and wind turbines. The attributes of light were considered, which can help us to see, feel happy, warm and comforted.)

Why did Jesus promise his friends that he would send his Spirit to them? God's Holy Spirit would be with all Jesus' friends, all through the ages, to guide and comfort and strengthen them; to fill them with the breath of the life of Jesus and the light of the love of Jesus. God's Spirit would always be with them to help them continue the work of Jesus in the world.

What was Jesus' special work? (The leader showed the children some of the 'Quadri Biblici' posters (see 'Visual aids' section of Resources at the back of the book) of Jesus' teaching and healing ministry and invited the children to identify what Jesus was doing in each picture.) Jesus showed his friends how to teach people about God, his Father, and how to show special love and care for the poor and sick people and the people nobody else cared about. So he promised them his Spirit, to live in them and complete Jesus' work.

When do we receive the Holy Spirit in a special way? At our baptism, when we became Jesus' friends, members of his family; and at Confirmation, when the Holy Spirit gives us the gifts we need to carry on the work of Jesus in the world.

When we were baptized, our own special baptism candle was lit from the paschal candle and one of our parents or godparents held the candle for us, if we were too tiny to hold it for ourselves. (The leader then lit the baptismal candle from the candle on the table.) The priest prayed that we would always keep the flame of Jesus' life and love burning brightly in our hearts. (The reader, helper and I

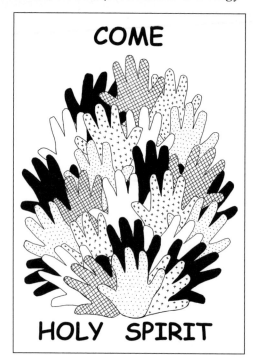

then gave each child a flame cut-out to hold and we each held a flame cut-out as well.)

Look at how many flames we are holding. These flames show us that the light of Jesus' life and love is with each of us.

Respond

Leader: We can't really go round all day holding a lighted candle or a flame cut-out to show others the light of Jesus in our lives, but how can we show the light of Jesus' life and love to others? (The leader had additional questions in mind in case it was necessary to draw out the children's ideas about how to show the light of Jesus at home, at school and at play.)

Let us each pray quietly in our hearts about what we are going to do this week to share the light of Jesus with others.

Who has Jesus promised to be with us to help us? (The Holy Spirit.)

We have a large poster here – what do the words say? (Come Holy Spirit.)

Let us stick all our small flame cut-outs on this poster to make one large flame and then we can take it into the church with us so that all the people can be encouraged to pray for God's Spirit to come into their lives in a new way. (The three adults, apart from the leader, helped the children to stick the flame cut-outs on to the poster, according to a prearranged design. Only the lower part of each flame needed to be glued, so that the tips of the flames gave a slightly 3D effect – see the illustration.)

Now let us stand and sing. (Some suggestions for music are given below.)

Suggestions for the song

- 'Share the Light' by Bernadette Farrell, *Share the Light*.
- 'Walk in the Light' (the children could join in the chorus, while the musician sings verses 1, 2, 4 and 6), *Laudate*, 771.
- 'Spirit – Friend', text Tom Colvin, arranged by Marty Haugen, tune Gonja folk song, adapted by Tom Colvin – *When Children Gather*.

Leader: After Mass, please tell your family about the story and the pictures that we talked about. Ask your family if they can show you your baptism candle and light it with you so that you can all pray together for the help of God's Spirit.

Go

When the signal is given a simple creed could be used, with a sung response such as 'We believe, we do believe', *Hymns Old and New*, 792.

Leader: Let us stand to sing about what we believe.

Musician: The response is 'We believe, we do believe.'

We believe in God, our Father. (Response)
We believe that he fills us with joy. (Response)
We believe in Jesus, the Son of God. (Response)
We believe he calls us to share his life and work. (Response)
We believe in the gift of God's Spirit to help us to live in the light of Jesus' love. (Response)

Leader: Let's pray our special intercessions.

God gave us the gift of life and he wants us to share in the life of Jesus, who has told us to ask God for what we need.
   We pray for all the young people who will soon receive the gifts of the Spirit in Confirmation. Spirit of Jesus . . .

Response: Come to us.

Leader: We pray for all the people who come to our church, that the Holy Spirit will help us to share the light of Jesus with other people. Spirit of Jesus . . .

Response: Come to us.

Leader: Loving Father, we love you and we thank you for listening to our prayers. Send your Holy Spirit to help us to follow Jesus and share in his work. We ask this through Jesus Christ, our Lord.

Response: Amen

Leader: We are now going to go back into the church to join our families and carry our lovely poster to where all the people can see it. (Before leaving the room, the helper extinguished the candle. The altar server led the procession down the side aisle, to the back. Two children carried the poster, while some other children carried the gifts. All the children processed up the aisle. The poster was presented to the priest, who asked an altar server to place it in front of the ambo. The priest thanked the children and told the congregation that the children's poster would be displayed from the Feast of the Ascension of the Lord until the eve of Pentecost, to mark the novena of prayer leading up to the great feast of the coming of the Holy Spirit. The children then returned to their families.

Commentary

The poster and flame cut-outs were ready for assembly, so completing the poster did not really encroach on the time for worship. Each child enjoyed watching their flame becoming part of the larger flame shape and delighted in the overall effect. The poster then had a use in the church for the novena leading up to Pentecost and could also be used during a separate children's liturgy of the word on Pentecost Sunday. If the poster is assembled directly on a fabric-covered board, then the flame cut-outs could each have Velcro on the lower part of the back, so that the large flame design can be assembled very simply and quickly. The same flame cut-outs can then be carefully removed during the Pentecost liturgy and held by each child to demonstrate that the Spirit came down on all the followers of Jesus.

8

A liturgy for Ordinary Time

A liturgy leader, a reader and a musician prepared and celebrated this children's liturgy of the word for the Fifteenth Sunday of Ordinary Time, Year A.

They chose as the focus: 'We pray that the seed of God's word will grow in our hearts.'

Resources

- A low table covered with a green cloth, a crucifix in a stand and a lighted candle.

- Four large seed trays filled with soil were placed on a plastic sheet on the floor. The first tray's soil was covered with flat stones, like small slabs, the second tray had some medium-sized stones partly embedded in the soil, the third tray had some weeds and pieces of thorn bush 'planted' in the soil and the fourth tray had only soil in it.

- A display of a flowering plant in a pot, some fruit and vegetables, a small sheaf of corn and a basket containing sunflower seeds was set up on another plastic sheet.

- A display board had some pictures taken from old calendars of corn and plants and shrubs growing in fields and gardens mounted on it.

- A poster of the sower.

- A few imitation birds (cut-outs or 3D models).

The liturgy was devised for children aged five to eight. The three members of the children's liturgy group prepared all the resources in advance and set up the liturgy room before the Mass.

Gather

See page 38 for details of arrangements to put in place before you and the children process to the liturgy room.

Leader: Let's put our special book of God's word on the table and sit down quietly on the floor. (The leader and reader sat on chairs either side of the table, while the musician sat by the keyboard.)

Do any of you know why we have come here? (The leader encouraged the children to put their hands up if they wanted to answer. She encouraged the children's responses, then summarized as follows.)

We have come here so that we can listen to God's word and be helped to understand God's message more easily. Are there some things here (gesturing towards the table) that are the same as in the church? (The Bible, table, cross, candle and flowers.)

Today we are going to think about the seed of God's word and how it can grow in our hearts. Let us begin by praising God for his goodness by standing up to sing 'Glory to God'. (The musician played and led one of the suggested versions of the gloria given on page 28.)

Listen

Leader: Look at the things on this sheet (gesturing to the display of plants, fruit, vegetables, wheat and seeds). What can you see? (The children identify the items and then their attention is directed towards the pictures on the display board and they are asked what they can see in each picture.)

What do seeds need if they are to grow into plants to give us flowers, fruit, vegetables and corn? (The children may need prompts to identify the need for soil, water, air, sunlight.)

Have any of you ever tried to grow a plant from a seed? What happened?

Today, our Gospel story is about a farmer who went out into his field to scatter some seed on the earth. It is a story that Jesus told his followers, a story with a message for them and for us. Let us stand up to welcome the Gospel. (The musician played the keyboard and led the singing of 'Feed Us With Your Word' by Paul Inwood in *Children at Heart*.)

Please sit down, and let's all listen very carefully as N. reads the Gospel story.

Reader: (Stood to proclaim the Gospel from the children's lectionary, Matthew 13:1–9.) A reading from the holy Gospel according to Matthew.

Jesus went out beside Lake Galilee, where he sat down to teach. Such large crowds gathered around him that he had to sit in a boat, while the people stood on the shore. Then he taught them many things by using stories.

He said: 'A farmer went out to scatter seed in a field. While the farmer was scattering the seed, some of it fell along the road and was eaten by birds. Other seeds fell on thin, rocky ground and quickly started growing because the soil was not very deep. But when the sun came up, the plants were scorched and dried up, because they did not have enough roots.

'Some other seeds fell where thorn bushes grew up and choked the plants. But a few seeds did fall on good ground where the plants produced a hundred or sixty or thirty times as much as was scattered. If you have ears, pay attention.'

This is the Gospel of the Lord.

Leader: Let's look at the poster of the sower – the farmer who went out to scatter the seeds on his field. What has he got over his shoulder? (A large bag.)

What do you think he was carrying in that large bag? (Seeds.) As he walked up and down his field, he threw handfuls of seed on to the ground.

(The leader gestured towards the four seed trays.) Here we have some trays showing different parts of the field that Jesus spoke about in the story. Who can tell me what these different parts of the field are?

(The leader then invited pairs of children in turn to scatter a small handful of the sunflower seeds on to each tray. She asked each pair of sowers in turn about their part of the field.) What's your part of the field like? When you tried to scatter some seeds, how many fell on to good soil? Do you think that any of the seeds will grow?

(To the first pair.) What did Jesus say about the birds? (This pair of sowers could then place the bird cut-outs or models on their piece of the field. They could be attached to short sticks, so that they can be set upright in the soil.)

What did Jesus mean when he talked about the seed in this story? Jesus told his followers that the seed is God's word, which he came to share with us. Some people did not listen to Jesus; they did not want to know about God's word. Their hearts were hard like rock.

Which part of the field is like that? (The path.)

Some people did listen to Jesus, but soon gave up trying to live God's word, so it did not take root in their hearts. Which part of the field is like that? (The stony part.)

Some people listened to God's word, but they were much more interested in other things, so God's word was pushed out of their lives by all those other things that they wanted. Which part of the field is like that? (The part with the weeds.)

Some people listened to God's word, they welcomed it into their hearts and they really tried to live as Jesus taught them. Which part of the field is like that? (The good soil.)

Which group of people are we like? Do we welcome God's word and want it to grow in our hearts? What can help God's word to grow in our minds and hearts? (Some additional prompts may be needed here. Hopefully the children will mention reading the Bible, listening to those who help us to understand God's word and praying to Jesus for help to live and love like him.)

As God's word grows in us, other people are able to see it grow because they can see that we are trying to live like Jesus.

Respond

Leader: Let us sit very quietly for a few moments and pray to Jesus in our hearts and tell him how we want to welcome God's word.

Now let us stand and sing. (The musician led one of the songs listed below.)

Suggestions for the song

- 'Listen to Jesus', Bernadette Farrell, *Share the Light*.
- 'Take The Word Of God With You', Christopher Walker, *Calling the Children*.

Leader: Please sit down again. As you leave the church at the end of Mass, we will give you a sheet like this to take home. On one side it has our Gospel story. Read it again at home or get a grown-up to read it with you.

On the back of the sheet is this picture. (The leader shows the children the picture, which is taken from page 97 of *The Complete Children's Liturgy Book* by Katie Thompson. The picture shows the sower and the four parts of the field mentioned in the Gospel story.) You may like to colour this picture in at home and tell your family how we tried to scatter the seeds like the sower.

How many of you have a children's Bible at home? During the week, you may like to read some Bible stories or get someone to help you read them, so that you can come to know more of God's word.

Go

When the signal was given by the altar server, the leader summarized very briefly, then said the following.

Leader: Let's stand and pray our special intercessions, just like the grown-ups are doing now in the church.

God gave us the gift of his word and he wants us to open our hearts to welcome it. Jesus has told us that God listens to our prayers, so let us ask him for what we need.

We pray that we will always listen to God's word and try to live like Jesus. Lord in your mercy . . .

Response: Hear our prayer.

Leader: We pray for our parents and priests and all those who help us to know and understand God's word. Lord in your mercy . . .

Response: Hear our prayer.

Leader: We pray for all families to grow in love. Lord in your mercy . . .

Response: Hear our prayer.

Leader: God our Father, we believe in your word. Please answer our prayers and help the seed of your word grow in our hearts. We ask this through Jesus Christ, our Lord.

Response: Amen

We are now going back into church to join our families. (Before leaving the room, the reader extinguished the candle. The altar server led the procession down the side aisle, to the back. Some children carried the gifts, as they all processed up the centre aisle and back to their families.)

Commentary

This liturgy requires quite a lot of preparation, especially getting the four seed trays ready. However, I believe it is a valuable way in which to help the children begin to understand the message of this parable. If there is time, the leader may need to recap the story and its meaning, in which case some more 'sowers' could be chosen to scatter a few more seeds.

Having a sheet for the children to take home also helps their parents to talk about the parable with their children. The particular picture I mentioned above is one that children enjoy talking about and explaining to their families.

I once saw this dialogue used during a Family Mass. The four large seed trays were raised up on a table, so that they were visible to people in the congregation. The children were invited forward to stand and listen to the Gospel and engage in the dialogue. After the Mass, I was fascinated to find five children looking intently at the seed trays. The older two were retelling the parable to the younger ones and explaining the meaning. It had obviously captured their interest and I was very impressed by the thoroughness of their presentation!

9

Viewpoints

The child's view

In our early experiences at Forest Row, although we had age ranges for the three groups of children, we were such a small community, with only 145 people at Sunday Mass, that, in practice, there was some flexibility. Children joined the youngest group for children's liturgy of the word as soon as they were happy to leave their parents and able to respect the stillness and prayerful atmosphere of the liturgy group. They moved on to the next age group when they felt ready and they stopped coming to the separate liturgy of the word as soon as they felt able to participate within the assembly. Then they were welcomed to share in one or more of the various liturgical ministries, as singers or musicians in the music group, in the ministry of welcome or as junior readers. Later on, they might decide to help with the youngest group for children's liturgy and, after Confirmation, become eucharistic ministers.

In their own separate liturgy, the children are able to hear God's word in a way that they can understand. The way in which the Gospel is introduced and its meaning shared enables children to listen with greater attentiveness and respond. They are also able to participate in the processions to and from their liturgy room, as well as the procession at Communion with a blessing for the younger ones, and this simple extra movement helps to exercise little limbs that may otherwise grow restless! Quite often, as a result, the children are attentive during the liturgy of the Eucharist as they have been given something to think about and look out for. Also, then, the rest of the Mass doesn't seem so long.

Whether the children go out or are called forward after the Gospel for a special dialogue within the assembly, their presence is recognized and participation welcomed, so they feel 'at home' in church, that they are important and they belong.

The parent's view

Every parent knows how tiresome it can be trying to get children ready for Mass. It only takes one reluctant or protesting child to make the whole family late and they then probably feel upset or annoyed on arrival at Mass. Over the years, many parents have told me that their children look forward to their own liturgy of the word and so are more keen to attend. This makes coming to Mass on Sunday far less stressful for parents and may encourage those who do not always come to attend more regularly.

Encouraging the children to tell their families after Mass or at home what their Bible story was about and what they did in their liturgy often encourages parents to share their faith with their children. If they have a worksheet to bring home or there is an item in the newsletter outlining the message the children were celebrating, this can also help parents to talk about the message of the Gospel. I know several parents who have found their way back to practising their faith or towards a new involvement in the parish as a result of helping their child in this way.

The priest's view

There are only a few times in the Mass when a priest celebrant can address the children especially. Moreover, some priests do not feel very confident holding a homily dialogue with children, so having members of the parish take on this role is very helpful. Having a separate liturgy of the word for the children means that their needs are not being neglected. This also puts less pressure on the priest celebrant in his role as presider over the whole assembly.

The priest calls the children forward and presents their lectionary to them and in that way identifies himself with what they are going to celebrate in their own liturgy room. The homily is the key to renewal and, while the children are sharing in a dialogue reflection, led by their liturgy leader, the priest can address his homily directly to the young people and adults in the church.

Over the course of a few years, children will be helped to listen to and explore the message of many Gospel passages during their own liturgy. This often results in children in the parish's First Communion programme having a good foundation of Bible stories, built up at home, at school and parish liturgy. If children are not learning this at home or school, the priest will be happy that they are able to receive it at church, knowing that this foundation makes sacramental preparation much easier.

The assembly's view

Whenever the children are especially involved during Mass, either within the assembly or celebrating their own liturgy of the word, most adults are delighted that the children's needs are being recognized and responded to. This is not to say that the children's needs should override those of any other group, but, when each group is being catered for, the assembly becomes a greater expression of the church as 'family'. Whenever there is a special dialogue for the children within the assembly or particular involvement of them – singing one of the chants, perhaps – the adults enjoy the children's participation and often say that they have found their dialogues illuminating.

The minister's view

Not surprisingly, the leaders especially, as well as the helpers, readers and musicians, find that this ministry challenges them to pray the scriptures and to find a greater richness in God's word. They may also be stimulated to read more about their faith and go on children's liturgy courses.

As a result of working with children, I have come to value the mutuality of ministry when children and adults worship together. The adults can give an impressive example by witnessing to their faith, holding out a sense of hope and expressing their love for the children in the assembly. Likewise children, with their rich resources of imagination, can bring a naturalness to the celebration as well as a sense of awe and wonder. Their uncomplicated participation can remind us of the childlike qualities that are required to experience the Kingdom.

Benefits for the children

The children feel that they belong, that their participation is welcomed. They are enabled to hear God's word and respond to it at their own level and are helped to make the transition from children's liturgy to adult liturgy.

Benefits for the parents

The parents are encouraged to attend Mass regularly because of their children's enthusiasm for taking part in the liturgy, if they don't already do so. The feedback parents receive from their children and the help they give their children when they bring home a worksheet helps parents to share their faith with their children.

Benefits for the priest

The priest, as presider over the whole assembly, is reassured that the children's needs are not being neglected. He is able to identify himself with what they celebrate in their own liturgy room without being under pressure to address the children's needs personally.

Benefits for the assembly

The assembly becomes a greater expression of the church as 'family' when the needs of the children as well as those of adults are recognized and catered for in appropriate ways.

Benefits for the ministers

The ministers discover new riches in God's word and are stimulated to discover more about their faith.

10

Reflections on the
Directory for Masses with Children

The *Directory for Masses with Children* (DMC – reproduced in full in Appendix 1) was first published in November 1973 as an official supplement to the Roman Missal. It was prepared following wide consultation with members of national liturgical commissions and was the fruit of years of discussion, enquiry and experiment. It deals with children's liturgical formation (see Glossary), Masses for adults in which children participate and those that are primarily for children, such as Masses for schoolchildren.

The DMC is concerned less with solutions for actual cases than principles and guidelines, exhortations and motivations, so it is necessary to have a clear understanding of the nature of liturgy as well as the function of liturgical law when applying this document to specific situations.

Sometimes the question is posed, 'Why cater for the children at all?' The *Constitution on the Sacred Liturgy* (CL) insists on the need for full, conscious, active participation of all, 'which the nature of the liturgy requires, and which, in virtue of their baptism, is the right and duty of the Christian people' (CL, 14). Children, as well as adults, share, through baptism, in the priesthood of Jesus Christ, yet today 'the circumstances of contemporary life in which children grow up are less favourable to their spiritual progress. In addition parents sometimes scarcely fulfil the obligations they accepted at the baptism of their children to bring them up as Christians' (DMC, 1). So, it is more important than ever that the whole Christian community helps its children by providing the means whereby they can fulfil their duty of worship and encounter Christ through liturgy.

The DMC proposes three different approaches towards adaptation of the ordinary parish Mass to meet the needs of children within the worshipping community: words only; actions and words; a special and separate liturgy of the word. At the very least, the presence of the children needs to be acknowledged 'by speaking to them directly in brief comments (as at the beginning and end of the Mass) and at some point in the homily' (DMC, 17). This may be done by the presider, addressing caring words of welcome to children during the Introduction, calling their attention to things that they should listen to or watch and so on. The priest may briefly summarize the message of God's word in images and language appropriate to the children's understanding and experience. Again, suitable words addressed to the children before the final blessing and dismissal could invite them to go forth to live and share the message of the word in their own special way. Regrettably, the presence of children at Mass is not always acknowledged like this.

Two means are proposed whereby children can be actively involved: bringing forward the gifts, ideally with their families, and singing one or other of the chants of the Mass (DMC, 18). Additional adaptations are permitted if considerable numbers of children are present. Then, the homily can be addressed specifically to the children, but in such a way that the adults too can profit by it (DMC, 19), and some of the adaptations suggested in Chapter 3 of the DMC may also be used.

In some parishes, I have seen the children invited up to stand round the altar during the eucharistic prayer. Maybe this is intended to draw them more closely into the offering of the whole assembly, but it can also become a source of distraction if the children are too young to grasp the solemnity of that part of the liturgy or cannot stay still and focused for that length of time. More meaningful involvement for the children happens when they are invited to gather round the sanctuary for the 'Our Father' and are encouraged to share the sign of peace as they return to their places. In many parishes, it is customary for the children who have not yet made their First Communion to come forward with their families in the procession to Communion to receive a blessing from the priest, deacon or eucharistic minister. The children enjoy processing and generally behave with dignity as they receive the blessing.

It is not necessary for children to understand everything that is going on in the Mass – indeed, who can ever completely comprehend the mystery of the Eucharist? However, we may fear for their spiritual harm unless the children can have a sense of belonging and be able to participate knowingly, actively and fruitfully and experience the love of God at work in their lives that we celebrate in liturgy. 'Children are capable of celebrating Eucharist. This is especially true when the words and signs of the liturgy are adapted. This does not mean that liturgy is trivialized or childish in its celebration. What it does mean is that pastoral care and liturgical action draw out children in their openness to mystery, the numinous and the mystical as well as the incarnational stories and images of God found in the Bible' (NDSW, p. 185).

The average parish celebration of Sunday Mass includes the aged, mature adults, young parents, adolescents, children, toddlers and infants. They come – with all their joys and sorrows, their needs and reasons for thanksgiving – to worship God. The worshipping community should, therefore, keep in view the needs of both adults and children and try to find a proper balance, neither ignoring the presence of children, nor permitting their interests to override those of others.

Children at Mass in small churches may feel closer to the action and more involved than those in larger church buildings, but, in both cases, the more they can participate in the action of the assembly, the more they will feel at home. There are important questions that must be considered concerning the needs of the children present at a liturgy primarily directed towards adults. Can they see the action of the sacred celebration? Can they sense simple dignity, grace, a certain self-discipline, some order and a lot of respect? Can they pray with the assembly? Can they participate in special dialogues? Can they sing acclamations, hymns, responses and psalms? Can they hear and understand the proclamation of the word? (See NDSW, pp. 193–4.)

Dissenting voices are beginning to make themselves heard, however, particularly in America, concerning the whole question of separating the children for their own liturgy of the word. Some stress that the child's place is within the assembly. For others, this is out-weighed by the advantages of being separated for a time, especially in situations where the liturgy of the word is 'celebrated so poorly that even adults fail to understand and be formed by it'. We must remem-ber that the DMC does not state that each and every Mass at which children are present should be adapted to their needs, but, 'if the fullest expression of the liturgical assembly is children and adults at prayer together, then we have no choice but to do whatever reveals this reality' (CAC, pp. 71 and 76).

The best scenario is to have a variety of Masses during the liturgi-cal year – some with a separate liturgy of the word and others with adaptations to meet children's needs, as well as Family Masses.

Masses where children remain with the community

Where children remain with the community throughout the Mass, on occasion a part of the homily can be made more particularly pertinent to them. In this chapter there are three homilies/dialogues and also an idea to use at the beginning of Lent.

The Jesse tree

During a Family Mass on either the Second or Third Sunday of Advent, when the Gospel passages refer to John the Baptist's role of preparing people to open their lives to the Messiah, the Jesse tree could be used as part of a homily primarily addressed to the children. (See the drawing at the end of this chapter.)

The priest leads the homily, with one or several readers – older children or teenagers – reading the script. Our priest used the first part of the homily time on the Third Sunday of Advent (Gaudete Sunday) to involve the children in the story of those who waited and longed for the coming of the Messiah and this was demonstrated by decorating the Jesse tree with figures and symbols of Old Testament characters.

The teenager who read the text paused at the end of each section to look across and observe the progress of the children placing the appropriate symbols and figures on the tree before resuming the narrative. The children were assisted by two liturgy helpers, as necessary, to secure their items to the right parts of the tree. The symbols were placed on the tree starting with the lowest branches, so that the

---

Resources

We used a 2-metre (6-foot) Christmas tree with thick, horizontal branches, firmly planted in a large tub, which, at the beginning of Mass, stood unadorned to one side of the front of the sanctuary.

The symbols mentioned in the script were in baskets, ready for distribution by the altar servers. We also used figures, with a name label on each, of the characters in the script — Abraham, Joseph, Moses, Jesse, David and Solomon. We had plenty of sheep for Jesse's symbol, so that every child would be sure to have one symbol or figure to bring forward at the appropriate time. Each symbol and figure had a loop of ribbon attached, so that it could easily be hung on the tree.

Before Mass, a star and a shell on a ribbon were hidden from view near the base of the tree by the liturgy helpers so that they could be produced at the appropriate time.

---

top branches were used for the symbols of Mary, Joseph and John the Baptist, with the star on the very tip of the tree. The strings of fig leaves (many leaf shapes were cut out of card and secured to a long string) and the string of stars were draped in spirals around the tree by the helpers. The priest used a hand-held microphone to pick up the children's responses.

During the Mass, after the Gospel, the priest invited all the children present, including toddlers assisted by a parent or grandparent, to come forward and sit on the sanctuary carpet. Stools were made available for adults accompanying toddlers and the priest sat on a stool near the children, who were near the ambo. The altar servers then distributed the symbols and figures from their baskets, keeping one symbol apiece for themselves.

The priest led the dialogue as follows.

Priest: Advent is a time of waiting for the birthday of Jesus. We all love to get ready for birthdays. We celebrate them with family and friends. Whose birthday do we celebrate on Christmas Day?

Today, we are going to get ready to celebrate Jesus' birthday by decorating Jesus' family tree – the Jesse tree. Jesse was the father of King David, one of the ancestors of Jesus. We will decorate the Jesse tree with symbols that remind us of some of the people who waited for Jesus to come.

Reader: We begin with Adam and Eve – the first man and woman. It was to them that God made his promise to send a Saviour. Their symbols are a snake and a string of fig leaves.

Next, we remember Noah. God saved Noah and his family and many animals from the flood. His symbols are a dove and a rainbow.

Abraham was chosen by God to be the father of God's special people. Because he trusted God, Abraham was promised by God that he would have many children and grandchildren who would wait for the coming of Jesus. God said that they would be as many as the stars in the heavens. Abraham's symbol is a string of stars.

Joseph was one of Abraham's grandsons. When he was young, Joseph's brothers sold him as a slave and he was taken to Egypt. Later, he was set free and became a leader in Egypt, where he helped God's people when there was no food in their own land. Jesus was to come to save all people. Joseph's symbol is a coat of many colours.

Moses led God's people out of Egypt. He received the ten commandments from God for his people. His symbols are a baby in a basket and a pair of sandals.

Jesse was the father of King David. Jesus was from the root of Jesse, whose family tree grew and grew. Many people waited for his coming. Jesse was a shepherd, so his symbol is a flock of sheep.

David was a king who loved God very much. He wrote many lovely prayers in songs, called psalms. We sing one at Mass every Sunday. King David came from Bethlehem, where Jesus would be born many years later. His symbol is a six-pointed star.

Solomon was also a king. He was wise and good. Solomon built a great church, called the temple, where God's people could come to worship God. His symbol is a crown.

We remember Jonah. Once, when he did not obey God, God sent a great fish to carry him to the place God wanted him to go. Jonah was inside the fish for three days, just as Jesus would be in the tomb for three days, before he rose from the dead. Jonah's symbol is a whale.

We now think of Joseph, the husband of Mary and foster father of Jesus. Joseph was a carpenter and so his symbols are a saw and a hammer.

Mary was chosen by God to be the mother of Jesus, the Saviour, whom everyone was waiting for. Mary's symbols are an angel, because God sent Angel Gabriel to Mary to ask her if she would be the mother of Jesus, and a lily, because God chose her to be born pure, free from sin.

Priest: About 2000 years ago, Jesus was born in Bethlehem. What symbol should we have for Jesus? (At first, some children suggested a cross, which he agreed was a good symbol, but then the priest asked what sign the wise men had followed to find their way to Jesus? The children then suggested a star and a liturgy helper stepped forward and put the star on top of the tree.)

Until Jesus was about 30 years old, most people did not know him. Then, his cousin started preaching to people near the River Jordan, asking them to change their ways and open their hearts to recognize Jesus as the long-awaited Messiah. What is the name of Jesus' cousin, whom I read about in today's Gospel? (John the Baptist.)

What symbol could we have for him? (A few suggestions from the older children included a locust and a pot of honey. When the priest asked what John was doing to the people when they stood before him in the water, the children said he was baptizing and some did the action of scooping and pouring water. When the other liturgy helper produced the shell, the children agreed that we could use it as a symbol, so she put it high up on the tree.)

Priest: How many days until Christmas? During the coming days, we shall all be waiting and getting ready to celebrate Jesus' birthday. Do you remember what happened when Mary and Joseph arrived in Bethlehem and were looking for a room where Jesus could be born?

Commentary

At first, some of the children were a little hesitant and looked rather unsure about what was expected, but, as the text unfolded, they soon got the idea and were quite excited when their symbol or figure was mentioned. In the distribution of the figures, the altar servers had been briefed to give them to children who would be able to read the name label or to toddlers accompanied by an adult. Only one toddler seemed reluctant to part with her symbol, offering at first her cuddly toy rather than the sheep from Jesse's flock that she was supposed to put on the tree!

There was a relaxed, joyful atmosphere during this part of the Mass (it was Gaudete Sunday after all!), which continued until the end of the celebration, and there were very many favourable comments from people of all ages. After Mass, the young children wanted to talk more about their symbol or figure and many people went to look at the tree more closely. The tree remained in the sanctuary during the Fourth Sunday of Advent and was then removed to the porch and redecorated as a Christmas tree.

The task of making the symbols and figures needs to be planned well in advance. People with artistic gifts need to be recruited and encouraged to make the items for the tree. Many of the symbols we used had been made by a group of young people who planned and worked together and, incidentally, had great fun doing so!

It is, of course, possible to include additional Old Testament characters in the text and use additional or different symbols to the ones given here. In fact, if this idea is used in successive years, you might feel the need to introduce variations to avoid repetition.

Giving the children a 'Christmas heart' to take home also reinforces the message to prepare our hearts to welcome Jesus into the family.

(The children told us that they could not find a room anywhere, that the innkeepers said no and Mary and Joseph ended up in a stable.)

The innkeepers did not find a place for Jesus, but do you think that we want to open our hearts and prepare a place in our hearts for Jesus to live in us? (Yes. He then showed the children A6-sized cards with a large heart shape on them and the instruction printed underneath, 'Please decorate this heart beautifully. Get someone to help you cut it out, then write your own special prayer of welcome to Jesus on the back. Finally, bring it to Mass on Christmas morning, when you will be able to bring it to the crib and read your prayer out, if you would like to.' He told the children that the 'Christmas heart' cards would be given out to them at the end of Mass. Finally, everyone was invited to look at how beautiful the tree had become and everyone clapped. He thanked the children and everyone who had taken part and helped to make the symbols for the tree. He also encouraged everyone, children and grown-ups, to look up some of the characters and stories shown on the Jesse tree in their Bibles at home.)

The Feast of Epiphany

This liturgy was written for the Family Mass on the Feast of Epiphany, which that year occurred on a Sunday (see also my book *Celebrating Advent and Christmas Liturgies with Young Children*. It would also be very suitable for a school Mass on the same feast day, whether it be celebrated in school or the local church. On such an occasion, perhaps the children's lectionary version of the Gospel may be used (see p. 76).

The hymn 'We three Kings' is suggested for the children's procession to the stable, when they follow the star. The star bearer needs to be quite tall and strong and it may be preferable to have two star bearers who take it in turns to carry the star aloft and hold it over the stable.

If children are in the majority in the assembly, such as at a school

---

Resources

- A large, silver star shape securely mounted on a long pole.
- A casket, such as a shiny biscuit tin, to represent the gift of gold, perhaps filled with chocolate coins covered in gold foil, which could later be given to the children.
- An empty thurible.
- An unbreakable jar, vase or other container to represent the myrrh.
- Cut-outs of the gifts of gold, frankincense and myrrh, preferably colour-coded (see the templates given at the end of this chapter).
- Several containers of pencils (short pencils, like the ones used for golf, are ideal).
- A large stable, represented, for example, by a large open clothes horse draped with hessian, with hay or straw and figures of Mary, Joseph and the Christ Child (unless children in costume and a baby or doll are to be used for these).
- Costumes, ideally, or at least headdresses, for the star-bearing angel, the three wise men, King Herod and Mary and Joseph.

Mass, it may be possible to use the following version of the Gospel (Matthew 2:1–12) from the *Lectionary for Masses with Children*.

Gospel reading

A reading from the holy Gospel according to Matthew.

When Jesus was born in the village of Bethlehem in Judea, Herod was king. During this time some wise men from the east came to

Jerusalem and said, 'Where is the child born to be king of the Jews? We saw his star in the east and have come to worship him.'

When King Herod heard about this, he was worried, and so was everyone else in Jerusalem. Herod brought together all the chief priests and the teachers of the law of Moses and asked them, 'Where will the Messiah be born?'

They told him, 'He will be born in Bethlehem, just as the prophet wrote, "Bethlehem in the land of Judea, you are very important among the towns of Judea. From your town will come a leader, who will be like a shepherd for my people Israel." '

Herod secretly called in the wise men and asked them when they had first seen the star. He told them, 'Go to Bethlehem and search carefully for the child. As soon as you find him, let me know. I want to go and worship him too.'

The wise men listened to what the king said and then left. And the star they had seen in the east went on ahead of them until it stopped over the place where the child was. They were thrilled and excited to see the star.

When the men went into the house and saw the child, with Mary, his mother, they knelt down and worshipped him. They took out their gifts of gold, frankincense and myrrh and gave them to him.

Later they were warned in a dream not to return to Herod, and they went back home by another road.

This is the Gospel of the Lord.

Dialogue

After the Gospel, it is desirable to invite all the children to come forward to sit at the front, on the floor facing the sanctuary. This dialogue would be led by a priest or deacon during an adult Mass in which children participate. If, however, it is celebrated at a children's Mass and only a few adults are participating, such as a school Mass, then a catechist, teacher or other lay person could lead the dialogue, especially if the priest finds it difficult to adapt himself to the mentality of children (DMC, 24). The children in costume remain at the side until they are called for.

Priest: In the Gospel story we have just listened to, what did the wise men follow to find their way to Jesus? (Hopefully they will mention the star. When they do, the priest asks the star bearer to bring the star so that it can be seen.)

Years ago, before people had maps and signposts, they used the positions of the sun and stars in the sky to tell them where they were. The wise men studied the stars and the things that were taught and written about God. They believed that this new star would guide them to where a new king had been born. What was special about this newborn king?

(The priest sends back the star bearer and calls for King Herod, if a child is to play this part.) When King Herod heard about the wise men and the questions they were asking about the newborn king, he sent for them. Why do you think Herod was worried? (Additional questions may be necessary to help the children to see that Herod feared for his position and power.)

King Herod told the wise men, 'Go to Bethlehem and search carefully for the child. As soon as you find him, let me know. I want to worship him too.' Did Herod really want to worship the newborn king? Did he have a different plan? What was his real plan?

King Herod had a wicked plan to kill the newborn king, Jesus, but the wise men had a good plan – they wanted to find Jesus and learn more about him. We are called by God to find out about Jesus and be like him.

(He sends back Herod and invites the wise men to come, carrying their gifts for the newborn king.) The first present the wise men gave to Jesus was gold. (The wise man with the gold shows the gift.) It is valuable and the wise men gave gold to Jesus to show that they believed he was a king. Jesus is a king, but not like kings who live in palaces and wear rich clothes. Jesus is king of love. He wants to be king of our hearts. (The gold is placed centrally, where it will remain until the procession to the stable at the end of the liturgy.)

The second present was called frankincense – a type of incense.

(The wise man with the thurible shows the gift.) When incense burns it gives a perfumed smoke. We use incense in church as a sign of our prayer rising to God. The wise men gave Jesus frankincense as a sign that they believed he was the Christ, the Holy One of God. (The thurible is placed beside the gold.)

The third present was myrrh. (The wise man with the myrrh shows the gift.) Myrrh is a perfumed ointment that was used to anoint people when they were sick and when they died. The wise men gave Jesus myrrh as a sign that they believed he would suffer and die for us. (The myrrh is placed beside the gold and the thurible and the wise men go to the side.)

Did you receive any presents at Christmas? We give presents to each other at Christmas as part of our way of celebrating Jesus' birth. I wonder if we thought about giving Jesus a present like the wise men did? Shall we each give him a present today? Let's think about it. (The priest invites the wise men to come forward, each carrying a basket containing sufficient of their respective paper cut-outs for all the children to have a choice.)

(He holds up a 'gold' cut-out.) If you want to give Jesus a gift like gold, you could promise to give a little of your pocket money to help feed a hungry child or to help some children in need.

(He holds up a 'thurible' cut-out.) If you want to give Jesus a gift like frankincense, you could promise to say a prayer for someone who needs us to pray for them – perhaps for someone who doesn't have anyone else to pray for them.

(He holds up a 'myrrh' cut-out.) If you want to give Jesus a gift like myrrh, you could promise to comfort someone you know who is sick – send them a 'get well' card or letter, telephone them or visit them with your family.

The priest may need to show each cut-out in turn once again and ask the children what gifts each represents. Then he should ask all the children to think about which gift they would like to choose. The wise men then need to give out their respective cut-outs accordingly. The pencils then need to be given out (a useful job for Herod and the angel, perhaps).

The priest should reassure the children that a little extra time will be allowed during the collection so that the adults can help the children to write their promise and/or their name on the back of their cut-out. However, before the children are sent from the sanctuary or worshipping space he says:

Priest: Thank you children, but, remember, later on the star will move and, when you see the star moving, follow it, just like the wise men did. Bring your cut-out, your present for Jesus, with you.

Where do you think the star will lead you to? Who will you find there?

When you reach the stable, go in one at a time and put your gift on the hay, just like the wise men did.

Commentary

The priest or deacon may wish to address a few words to the adults present, following the dialogue with the children. In any case, the invitation to make a commitment to offer a gift to the Lord should prompt adults, as well as the children, to decide to make a specific offering to celebrate this great feast.

When we celebrated this liturgy during the Family Mass on the Feast of Epiphany, which, that year, was on a Sunday, there was a very happy atmosphere throughout. Each child was very serious about writing their message on their chosen cut-out, but this activity did not extend beyond the time of the collection and procession of gifts. Most children were watching and waiting attentively for the star to move so that they could follow it.

Again, people need to be recruited in advance to prepare all the cut-outs (the templates for them are given at the end of this chapter). It is a task that a few senior or housebound parishioners could be invited to do – they are often delighted to be involved, especially in something that helps the children.

The star bearer and wise men need to be briefed so that, once the singing of 'We three kings' begins, the star is raised up and carried slowly to the stable by a long route. The wise men collect their gold, frankincense and myrrh and follow. The rest of the children will join them, hopefully!

If children are to play the parts of Joseph and Mary, they may need someone to prompt them as to when they should enter the stable with the baby so that they are there when the wise men and the children arrive. The carol is, in fact, intended to be sung at the end of Mass, as the final hymn, so it is only at the end that the children follow the star to the crib and present their gifts.

The parable of the rich man and Lazarus

This reading, from Luke 16:19–31, is proclaimed on the Twenty-sixth Sunday of Year C, which is just prior to CAFOD Harvest Fast Day. I have celebrated this with children in three ways:

- using two large, doubled-sided faces on bamboo poles, held by older children (see the drawings at the end of this chapter)
- using children in costume dressed up as the rich man (and perhaps his servant) and Lazarus (and perhaps a helper)
- during a separate children's liturgy using two large posters with the outline of the rich man and of Lazarus on them, and a series of clothes and objects (such as a cup of wine for the rich man and a begging bowl for Lazarus) as well as a dog cut-out that the children could stick on to the outlines, using Velcro, as the story is being discussed.

The two large, double-sided faces work well, even in a large church, and the two children holding them could also have large name labels on to identify them as the rich man and Lazarus, respectively. If some of the children are dressed up as the characters, Lazarus could wear opaque, flesh-coloured tights under his poor ragged garment, daubed with brown and red paint to indicate dirt and sores.

CAFOD envelopes or boxes need to be ready to offer to the adults and children at the end of Mass.

If the dialogue that follows below is used during a Family Mass, the celebrant may permit the use of the version of the Gospel from the children's lectionary – possibly even the abridged version I have included below (Luke 16:19–25). If this Gospel is to be used at a children's Mass, in school for example, or during a separate children's liturgy, then the abridged version would be appropriate, especially for younger children.

Gospel reading

A reading from the holy Gospel according to Luke.

Jesus told his disciples this story: 'There was once a rich man who wore expensive clothes and every day ate the best food. But a poor beggar named Lazarus was brought to the gate of the rich man's house. He was happy just to eat the scraps that fell from the rich man's table. His body was covered with sores, and dogs kept coming up to lick them. The poor man died and angels took him to the place of honour next to Abraham.

'The rich man also died and was buried. He went to hell and was suffering terribly. When he looked up and saw Abraham far off and Lazarus at his side, he said to Abraham, "Have pity on me! Send Lazarus to dip his finger in water and touch my tongue. I'm suffering terribly in this fire." Abraham answered, "My friend, remember that while you lived, you had everything good, and Lazarus had everything bad. Now he is happy, and you are in pain." '

This is the Gospel of the Lord.

Dialogue

After the proclamation of the Gospel, it may be desirable to invite all the children to come forward to sit at the front, on the floor, facing the sanctuary. This dialogue would be led by a priest or deacon during an adult Mass where children participate. If, however, it is celebrated at a children's Mass that only a few adults will attend, such as a school Mass, then a catechist, teacher or other lay person could lead the dialogue. The children holding the large double-sided faces on poles, or the children in costume, remain at the side until the priest calls for them.

Priest: In the Gospel we have just listened to, Jesus told a story to his friends. It's only a story, but Jesus often used stories to help people to understand God's word. Children, with your help, I would like us to find the message in this story.

What was the rich man's life like when he was alive? Did he have a lovely house, fine clothes, plenty of food? Do you think that he had servants to do all the housework? (If children in costume are used, the rich man, together with his servant, perhaps offering him a bowl of fruit or goblet of wine, could come forward and stand on one side of the priest.) Do you think he was happy then?

If, instead, the large faces on bamboo poles are to be used, the child holding the pole representing the rich man's face could come forward, holding the pole to show the 'happy' face, and stand on one side of the priest.

What was the poor man's life like when he was alive? Where did he live? Did he have fine clothes, plenty of food? What did the dogs do to him? (If children in costume are used, Lazarus (helped by his friend, perhaps) could come forward and sit on the other side of the priest.)

Do you think that he was happy then? (If, instead, the large faces on bamboo poles are to be used, the child holding the pole representing Lazarus' face could come forward and hold the pole to show the 'sad' face, standing on the other side of the priest.)

What happened when the rich man died? Where did he go? (If children in costume are used, the rich man should collapse to a crouching position and look very sad. (His servant would walk off at this point, carrying the bowl of fruit or goblet of wine.) Do you think he was happy then?

(If, instead, the large faces on bamboo poles are to be used, the child holding the pole representing the rich man's face should swivel the pole, to present the 'sad' face to the children and the congregation.)

What happened when the poor man died? Where did he go? Was he happy then? (If children in costume are used, Lazarus should stand up, with his arms raised and look very happy. His helper would walk off at this point.)

Do you think he was happy then? (If, instead, the large faces on bamboo poles are to be used, the child holding the pole representing Lazarus' face should swivel the pole to present the 'happy' face to the children and the congregation.)

Was there any way in which both men could have been happy at the same time? (Hopefully, the children will suggest that if the rich man had shared with Lazarus before he died, they could both have been happy at the same time. If children in costume are used, the two remaining 'actors' could come together in the middle of the sanctuary and hold hands. If a child is acting as the servant, that child could come to the rich man and offer the fruit and wine, which he could offer to Lazarus, who could, in turn, summon his helper to share the fruit and wine as well.) If, instead, the large faces on bamboo poles are to be used, the child holding the pole representing the rich man's face should swivel the pole, to present the 'happy' face to the children and the congregation, so that both faces are now showing their 'happy' side.)

So, children, what's the message that Jesus was telling his friends and telling us? Jesus said, share what you have with those who need your help.

Now, before the children return to sit with their families, the priest could address the adults, talking about sharing some of what we have, via the CAFOD Harvest Fast Day envelopes, with those who, each day, have to cope with the anxiety of trying to find a little food, water, shelter or medicine for their families. The priest thanks all the children for helping everyone to understand the message of Jesus, then the children return to their places with their families.

Commentary

This story, with its references to life after death, can be difficult to explain to young children, but its message can be brought to life when children in costume, or the large double-sided faces, are used. The faces need to be large (about 35–45 cm – 14–18 in in diameter) in order to be clearly seen in a large church.

The use of 'actors' or such visual aids makes the Gospel story memorable for all. The children who are going to act would only need one practice, ideally with whoever is to lead the dialogue. One year, the 'faces' could be used, and 'actors' could be used the next time this reading occurs in the cycle of readings, which will be three years later. The dialogue could also be used during a class or school Mass or separate liturgy of the word.

The First Sunday of Lent

On the First Sunday of Lent, there could be a brief dialogue with the children about Lent during the homily, if the children remain with the community, or during their own separate liturgy of the word. Then, all the children could be presented with a lenten cross cut-out or an A5-size card with the lenten cross design on it (see the template at the end of this chapter) before the blessing.

The lenten cross has 40 triangular shapes in it – one for each day of Lent. The dialogue could focus on asking the children for ideas about how to grow in love during Lent; how to live more like Jesus and love more like Jesus. The emphasis should be on what to do, not just on what to give up. If children offer ideas about giving up sweets or crisps, let's say, then the dialogue could pursue the idea of what to do with the money saved by not buying those items.

The lenten cross can be used in various ways

- Each time the child does something to grow in love, they can colour in a triangle on their cut-out.
- They can draw a symbol or write a word in a triangle.
- If they have an A5-sized card, instead of a cut-out, they could colour in a triangle and write what they did on the back of the card.
- The children could also be invited to bring their lenten crosses back to church on Good Friday, to put them in a basket near the cross, when they take part in Veneration of the Cross.

Eucharistic Prayers for Masses with Children

There are three eucharistic prayers in *Eucharistic Prayers for Masses with Children* (see Resources at the end of this book). One of these could be chosen by the celebrant for use during a First Holy Communion Mass, special Masses for children and school Masses (see especially the Introduction, where the liturgical use of these prayers is explained). While their use is limited to Masses celebrated with children, it is important to know that they exist and have a value in helping children to follow and participate in the eucharistic prayer, for they have been written in a simpler style of language and include opportunities for the children, especially, to respond in song using various acclamations.

A Jesse tree

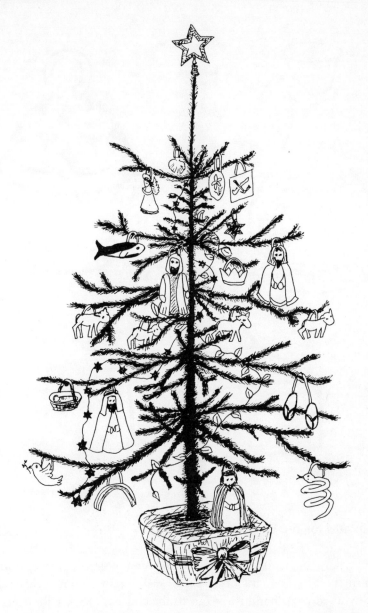

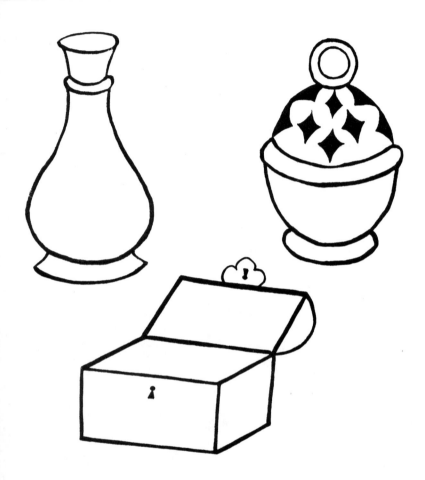

Templates for the Epiphany liturgy

Make enlargements of these to A5 size using a photocopier, printing each of the three designs on paper of a different colour – this helps when you come to hand them out to the children. Seek volunteers to help you cut out each shape.

The faces for the rich man and Lazarus

Use paper in a bright colour, such as orange, for the circle for the happy face and an unhappy colour, such as mauve, for the sad face.

A lenten cross

12

Liturgies other than Masses

When planning a liturgy for use with children that is not at a Mass, it is just as important to keep the shape of liturgy we have used throughout – gather, listen, respond, go – and the general principles of liturgy in view.

Some liturgical principles

- Liturgy is action and symbol. It speaks to the whole person, involving all the senses – sight, touch, hearing, taste and smell.
- In liturgy, we discover the riches of prayer, through word and gesture, silence and stillness.
- The purpose of adapting liturgy for children is to lead them into full, conscious and active participation in the liturgy of the parish.
- Liturgy with children, as with adults, demands dignity, clarity and simplicity.

I now offer three examples of liturgies for children other than Mass. These are a liturgy for Holy Thursday, First Reconciliation and an Advent Family Reconciliation liturgy.

A liturgy for Holy Thursday

This liturgy was devised for younger children who would not normally attend the evening Mass of the Lord's Supper on Holy

Thursday. It may be led by a priest, deacon or lay person. Young families who belong to other Christian traditions where Sunday Eucharist is celebrated regularly may find that this is a liturgy they would be happy to share in, so it could be planned and celebrated ecumenically.

The celebration could take place in the church or a large hall. If the

Resources

- A low table.
- Three children, boys and girls, in costume, who have rehearsed beforehand, to play the parts of Jesus, Peter and John.
- A coloured cloth, two candles in suitable glass holders that are safe to have alight near children, a pottery chalice and a ciborium dish with a round pitta bread on it. All these items are hidden near the sanctuary to be brought on when needed by the children playing Peter and John.
- A children's lectionary, with the Gospel reading marked, and a reader.
- Matches, held by a liturgy helper.
- A large basket or other container holding sufficient large pitta breads, each sealed in a plastic bag, to be distributed to each family as they leave.
- A pottery jug of water, a large pottery basin and a towel, which are also kept hidden until needed.
- Sufficient A6-sized cards printed with one or more designs, such as a suitable clip art picture or design, on one side and blank on the other.
- Sufficient pencils to distribute to the children when they need to write on their chosen card.
- A music group.

church is the venue, then the table used could be placed in the sanctuary area near to the congregation, preferably up some steps, so that the area in which it is situated could be considered to be the Upper Room. If children in wheelchairs or with other special needs are taking part, then a hall or large area without steps might be better.

The actors and reader are seated at the side of the sanctuary or other worshipping space before the liturgy begins. All the other children sit with their families at the beginning of the liturgy. Just before the liturgy begins, it is important to tell all the parents present that the children, who volunteer and are chosen to act as the other disciples at the Last Supper, will be offered a piece of pitta bread to eat. This is to guard against selecting a child for whom eating pitta bread would be harmful to their health, but the other children who take part will not be given anything to eat or drink, so no child will be excluded.

Suggestions for the opening song

- 'You have called us', by Bernadette Farrell, *Share the Light*.
- 'The night before our Saviour died' by Damien Lundy, *Hymns Old and New*, 538, verses 1 and 2.

Welcome and introduction

The priest or lay presider welcomes everyone and explains that the liturgy has been prepared so that the children can play a special role in it. If members of other Christian communities are taking part, a special welcome is given to them.

Opening prayer

God our Father,
We are gathered here to remember what Jesus, your Son, did at the Last Supper, to show us his great love. Help us to open our hearts

now to your word and to grow in love, through Jesus Christ, our Lord.

Response: Amen

Gospel acclamation

See page 27 for suggestions.

Gospel reading

A reading from the holy Gospel according to Mark. (Mark 14:12–16, 22–26)

It was the first day of the Feast of Thin Bread, and the Passover lambs were being killed. Jesus' disciples asked him, 'Where do you want us to prepare the Passover meal?'

Jesus said to two of the disciples, 'Go into the city, where you will meet a man carrying a jar of water. Follow him, and when he goes into a house, say to the owner, "Our teacher wants to know if you have a room where he can eat the Passover meal with his disciples." The owner will take you upstairs and show you a large room furnished ready for you to use. Prepare the meal there.'

The two disciples went into the city and found everything just as Jesus had told them. So they prepared the Passover meal.

During the meal Jesus took some bread in his hands. He blessed the bread and broke it. He gave it to his disciples and said, 'Take this. It is my body.'

Jesus picked up a cup of wine and gave thanks to God. He then gave it to his disciples and said, 'Drink it!' So they drank it.

Then he said, 'This is my blood, which is poured out for many people, and with it God makes his agreement. From now on I will not drink any wine, until I drink new wine in God's kingdom.'

Then they sang a hymn and went out to the Mount of Olives.

This is the Gospel of the Lord.

Dialogue

This may be led by a priest, deacon or liturgy leader – preferably some-one who is familiar to the children. The children remain in their places with their families until they are chosen to take part in the acting. In a large building, the person leading the dialogue may need to wear a lapel microphone and carry a hand-held microphone to pick up the children's responses. The leader of the dialogue, who could be the same person as the one who is presiding, needs to walk round among the children in all parts of the building to listen to their answers.

Leader: In the Gospel story, we have just heard that Jesus sent two of his disciples to go and prepare the special Passover meal for Jesus and his friends. Do any of you know their names? (Peter and John. The leader then introduces the two children who will act the parts of Peter and John.)

Who were they to look out for and follow? (A man carrying a jar of water.)

When they were preparing the table for the meal, what do you think they needed? (Prompting-type questions may be needed to elicit the responses – tablecloth, food and drink. As the cloth, candles, bread and wine are mentioned, Peter and John set them on the table, while a liturgy helper lights the candles.)

They had no electricity in those days and it was evening time, so what did they need for light? (Candles.)

What special food and drink did Jesus use? (Bread and wine.)

The bread that the Jews use for the Passover meal is called un-leavened, or 'thin', bread. We will use pitta bread in this celebration.

(The leader introduces the child who is to act the part of Jesus.) Jesus had a group of special friends called the apostles. How many apostles shared the meal with Jesus? (Twelve.)

We already have Peter and John, so how many more do we need? (Ten. Volunteers are sought and ten are chosen. Jesus and the apostles sit on the floor round the table, with Peter and John on either side of Jesus.)

When Jesus took the bread, what did he say? What did Jesus say about the cup of wine? (Then Jesus takes the bread and the cup and says the words, breaks the pitta bread into pieces and shares them with the apostles, who eat the pitta bread. Then the cup is shared. Diluted squash that looks like red wine could be used in the cup, but it may not be desirable for the children to drink from the same cup because of hygienic or dietary considerations. If so, drinking from the cup could be mimed.)

What happened to Jesus the next day? (Jesus was crucified.) Was his death the end of the story? (No.) What happened on Easter day? (Jesus rose from the dead.) After Jesus had been seen, risen from the dead, by his friends, where did he go after 40 days? (Back to his Father in heaven. Jesus walks away to sit somewhere out of sight.)

Who took Jesus' place after he went back to heaven? (Peter.) Peter now takes the place of Jesus at the special meal. Each Sunday – the day that Jesus rose from the dead – the friends of Jesus met together to remember Jesus and Peter did what Jesus had done at the Last Supper. (Peter mimes what Jesus did with the bread and the cup.)

Gradually they all got older and older . . . and then they all died. (The apostles walk round the table, acting like very old people, then they lie down on the floor pretending to die.)

Well, if that was what happened, that would mean the end of Jesus' group of friends – the Church! But that wasn't what really happened. What did they do to find more friends of Jesus before they died? (The children suggest that the apostles went out and told people about Jesus.) In fact, that is what they did, so come alive again and each go out to bring in a new disciple. (The apostles go into the congregation and each return with a child or older person who agrees to become a friend of Jesus. They all gather round the table and Peter again mimes what Jesus did at the Last Supper.)

So when Peter and the first disciples died, the new disciples went out to find more disciples. (The original 12 walk off and the new recruits go into the congregation and each return with a new friend of Jesus. Then all these can be sent off again to find a new recruit each, so that eventually all the children and some of the adults are gathered round the table.)

This work of going out and telling people about Jesus and inviting them to be his friends and share in his special meal continued all through the years, down to today.

Who first told you about this special meal in memory of Jesus? Who first brought you to it? When we come together on Sundays, or on weekdays, to share in this special meal, who takes the place of Jesus for us here? (If any of the priests are present, they can be invited forward to sit at the head of the table.)

Why did Jesus give his friends (that means us as well) his body and blood? (To show his love and to let us share his life.) Jesus wants to be with us always. He wants to show us his love and let us share in his own life.

(The presider thanks all the children for taking part. They are invited to return to their families and then everyone responds in song. Here are some ideas.

Suggested songs

- 'We Remember You' and
- 'God's Greatest Gift', both by Bernadette Farrell, *Share the Light*.
- 'No Greater Love' by Mark Friedman and Janet Vogt, *Behold the Lamb*.
- 'Jesus, I Love You' by Sister Rosalie Vissing, *Hymns Old and New*, 278.

At the end of the song, Peter and John bring out the jug of water, basin and towel and place them where everyone can see them, near the table.)

Some of the children have just acted out what Jesus did during that special meal that Jesus shared with his friends. Before the meal, Jesus took a towel and wrapped it round his waist. Then he poured water into a basin and began to wash the feet of his friends. Peter did not think it was right that Jesus should wash his feet, because Jesus was their leader, but Jesus said that he wanted to wash their feet to show his love and friendship with each of them. So Peter let Jesus wash his feet.

It was the work of one of the servants to wash the feet of those invited to the meal, so why did Jesus do it? What was he trying to show his friends?

Jesus asked his friends to follow what he had done and act like servants to each other. In what ways can we serve others – at home, at school, at play?

The leader encourages the children to give their ideas about serving others. Then, he or she shows the children the cards that have been prepared for them and on the back of which they are to write their own prayer – a prayer promising to help someone in a special way at home, at school or at play. The actors Jesus, Peter and John could give out the cards and the pencils for the children to write their prayers. When the children have finished, they are invited to come forward to place them in a basket that the presider holds in front of the table. During this time, the music group could sing any of the songs given below.

Suggested songs for the music group

- 'The Servant King' by Graham Kendrick, *Laudate*, 749.
- 'Servant Song' by Richard Gillard, harmony by Betty Pulkingham, *Laudate*, 924.
- 'Washing Feet' by Mark Friedman and Janet Vogt, *Behold the Lamb*.

Then the basket is placed in front of the table and everyone stands to join in the Our Father. This is followed by the invitation to offer each other the sign of peace.

Commentary

This liturgy, which is usually held on Holy Thursday afternoon, is popular with families with young children because all the children can join in. Even though young children may not understand the full meaning of the Eucharist, they can begin to understand something of the idea of Jesus' friends coming together to share a special meal.

The Gospel account in Mark of the preparation of the Upper Room and the institution of the Eucharist is given in the children's lectionary, but not John's account of the washing of the feet. That is why Mark's Gospel is given as the reading for the liturgy and the leader simply tells the story of the washing of the feet. (This matches up with the readings at the Mass of the Lord's Supper as, in the second reading, Paul writes to the church at Corinth of the Institution of the Eucharist, while the Gospel reading is John's account of the washing of the feet.)

At the time when the washing of the feet is spoken of, this could be done by the presider in the same way that it would be done during the Mass of the Lord's Supper.

If the children have been saving some money during Lent for the poor and needy, they could be encouraged to bring their offerings to the liturgy and these could be brought up as well as, or instead of, their prayer offerings on cards. Also, instead of using the concluding prayer that is given here, those children who wish could read out their prayers before placing them in the basket.

Concluding prayer

God, our Father,
we thank you for the example of Jesus, who washed the feet of his friends and gave us the command to love and serve one another.

Help us to serve one another lovingly, especially in our families. We ask this through Jesus, the Lord.

Response: Amen

Following a blessing (or the grace), everyone joins in a concluding song, such as one of those listed below.

Suggestions for the concluding song

- 'Though We are Many/Make us a Sign' and
- 'Share the Light of Jesus', both by Bernadette Farrell, *Share the Light*.
- Any of the other songs suggested in this liturgy not already included.

Then, as everyone leaves, each family is given a pitta bread to take home and share.

A celebration of the gift of forgiveness

Despite our contemporary understanding of children's moral development pointing to their inability to commit serious sin or make a formal confession, the current requirement for children to celebrate First Reconciliation before First Holy Communion remains. Ideally, beginning with the experience of saying sorry, forgiving other people, being forgiven and making peace in the family, children should be led to a deepening of their understanding and experience of conversion (that is, changing our ways) and reconciliation and be helped to celebrate the Sacrament of Reconciliation when they have sufficient spiritual maturity. Although some children in a First Holy Communion group may be approaching such a level of maturity, others may not. Therefore, the liturgy used needs to include and involve all the children in the group, as well as their siblings and parents, some of whom may not be Catholics. It needs to make provision for participants to receive sacramental absolution, a prayer for healing or a blessing according to their need and disposition. The title of this liturgy – celebration of the gift of forgiveness – expresses its inclusive nature, for we can all praise and thank God for his gifts of forgiveness and peace.

This liturgy is intended to be celebrated with a small group of

---

Resources

- Sufficient posters from the 'Quadri Biblici' series or similar series, one for each First Holy Communion group child. The posters selected need to portray the nativity, Jesus teaching, blessing the children, healing people and working miracles, such as feeding the multitude, as well as his death and resurrection. It is also necessary to include the poster showing Jesus inviting Zacchaeus to come down from the tree. The children need to have become well acquainted with these posters and the stories they depict during their First Holy Communion group sessions. The posters need to be distributed so that each child has one, face upwards on the floor in front of them, before the liturgy begins.

- A children's lectionary, with the Gospel reading marked. Also needed is a reader – a catechist, helper or parent.

- Liturgy booklets, so that everyone can follow and join in.

- A musician or music group would be ideal, but, if necessary, the singing can be led using a cassette or CD for the songs and also for gentle music during the time of individual ministry.

- A tray with containers of lead pencils, colouring pencils, a few erasers and sharpeners.

- Each priest needs a small basket with prayer cards that he will give to each child at the end of their chat with him.

children, ideally not more than 12. It needs to be celebrated in a large space, with areas available where the priests can offer individual ministry and still be visible, yet not so close to the group that they could be overheard.

The children in the First Holy Communion group sit in a circle in the middle of the space, on a carpet or carpet squares. At least three priests are needed, depending on the planned size of the group participating.

It is important that the liturgy does not last more than 30 to 45 minutes, otherwise the children will become restless. Also, if the adults sense that people have to queue for quite a time, they may give up on the idea of seeking individual ministry.

The priests, parents, other family members, catechists and helpers sit on seating arranged around the circle of children. In between the outer and inner circle, you may decide to arrange a large paper chain with coloured links, symbolizing the circle of love – the love we are called to show for God and other people. If such a paper chain circle is used, its significance needs to be referred to by the presider at some point in the celebration, maybe at the beginning or before the Our Father.

Having some background music playing helps to set the mood as the children and their families gather. It may be necessary to practise

---

Suggestions for the opening song

- 'Circle Song' by Bernadette Farrell, *Share the Light*.
- 'A New Commandment', *Laudate*, 920.
- 'We Hear God's Word' by Christopher Walker, *Calling the Children*.
- 'We Come as Servants' by Mark Friedman and Janet Vogt, *Enter the Journey*.
- 'If I Am Lacking Love' by Damien Lundy, *Hymns Old and New*, 232.

one or more of the songs that will be used during the celebration. Although the songs chosen will be familiar to the children, the parents and priests may not know them and, in such an intimate celebration, it is important that everyone can join in.

Welcome and greeting

The presiding priest offers kind words of welcome. He introduces the other priests present, if they are not known, and starts the liturgy.

Priest presider: In the name of the Father, and of the Son and of the Holy Spirit.

Introduction

Priest presider: Jesus showed God's love to everyone and asked his followers to love others just as he loved them. When people fail to love or turn away from the light of God's truth, Jesus gives them God's gift of forgiveness as they turn to him in sorrow.

Opening prayer

Priest presider: God our Father,
we thank you for the great love that you have for each one of us. In your love, you have called each of us into your family to share in your life and your love. We thank you for sending Jesus, your dear Son, to show us your love. Help us, now, to open our hearts to your word and welcome your gift of forgiveness that makes things right. We ask this through Jesus Christ, our Lord.

Response: Amen

Gospel acclamation

See the suggestions on page 27.

Gospel reading

Reader: A reading from the holy Gospel according to John. (John 13:34–35)

Jesus said to his disciples: 'I am giving you a new command. You must love each other, just as I have loved you. If you love each other, everyone will know that you are my disciples.'

This is the Gospel of the Lord.

Dialogue

This may be led by one of the priests, a catechist or liturgy leader, but preferably someone who is familiar to the children and ideally someone who knows each child by name.

The leader of the dialogue explains that the children are going to tell everyone, using their posters, how Jesus showed love to people. Then, starting by holding up the nativity poster, the leader explains that Jesus showed love by coming down to earth to teach us about God and show us the way to heaven. Each child is then invited, by name, to hold their poster up and explain it. This ensures that the narrative follows a reasonably chronological sequence. It may be necessary to ask a few extra questions, but any child who has an answer may be invited to help another to explain. The leader thanks the children for their answers.

The priest presider continues as follows.

Priest presider: Sometimes people do not love others as well as Jesus did. Older people, such as Zacchaeus in the poster we saw a few moments ago, can behave in a way that is unjust and hurts others. When anyone who has not loved as Jesus showed us turns to God and says sorry, God shows his unending love by giving them his gifts of forgiveness, healing and peace. Let us be still for a few moments to think about how we have made 'ripples of love', sharing God's love with others, and let us think as well about any ways in which we have not loved as Jesus asks us to.

Prayer of sorrow

The priest presider leads everyone in saying this prayer, slowly, together.

Dear God,
I thank you for loving me and for calling me to live in love. Help me to learn from Jesus how to love him and other people as much as he loves me. If I have failed to love, I am sorry, and I ask you to share with me your gift of forgiveness, so that I can also try to forgive others. Please help me to grow in love.

Response: Amen

Invitation

Priest presider: The priests stand in the place of Jesus and so each person is invited to go to one of them to ask for the gift of God's forgiveness, if they need it, or to ask for a blessing or receive a word of encouragement to help them to grow in love. (The priest presider indicates where each priest will be seated in suitable places around the church or other space.) I encourage parents to bring their children to the particular priest the children would like to talk to and remain nearby, out of earshot but within sight of their children. Once each child has talked to a priest, I encourage parents and other family members to do the same. Your children will be well looked after by their catechists and helpers back in the circle.

The priests will give the children cards on which they can write their own special prayers to thank God for the gift of forgiveness. While all this is happening, there will be gentle music playing. While you may be waiting to talk to a priest, please pray for your family and one another.

Response

While the children are being taken to the priest of their choice, the catechists and helpers collect up the posters and bring the tray of pencils into the centre of the circle. Then the children of the First Holy Communion group, and their siblings, return to the circle with the cards the priests have given them. Each child can be encouraged and helped by their catechists and liturgy helpers to compose their own prayer of thanks on their card and then decorate the border using colouring pencils. Throughout this time, suitable music can be played, which will help to preserve a prayerful atmosphere even when the children are preparing their prayer cards.

Our Father and the sign of peace

When everyone has returned to the inner or outer circle, the priest presider invites everyone to stand and maybe hold hands in their circle as the Our Father is prayed together. Then everyone is invited to share the sign of peace.

Prayers of thanksgiving

Everyone sits down and the children are invited to take it in turns to read out their prayers, if they wish. The priest presider thanks the children and then invites everyone to stand for the concluding prayer.

Concluding prayer

Priest presider: Loving Father,
thank you for your gift of forgiveness and for making things right. Help us to grow in love and, through the power of your Holy Spirit, make us living signs of your love for the whole world to see. We ask this through Christ our Lord.

Response: Amen

Suggestions for the concluding song

- *Share the Light of Jesus*, by Bernadette Farrell.
- 'Sing Hosanna', *Laudate*, 772 (also known as 'Give me joy in my heart').
- 'O Lord, all the World Belongs to You' by Patrick Appleford, *Laudate*, 847.

If the necessary facilities are available, this celebration can be followed by simple refreshments.

Commentary

Celebrating this liturgy with a small group of families helps everyone to feel special, but particularly those children in the First Holy Communion group.

A good ratio of priests to people helps the liturgy to flow and not run on too long.

Participants have had very positive feelings about this liturgy, finding it to have been an enjoyable, happy occasion for the children – refreshingly different from most of the parents' recollections of their experiences of First Confession!

This liturgy can be adapted to be celebrated as a Penitential Service for children without a priest presider. A Penitential Service is a liturgy of sorrow and repentance without absolution for sin. It is recommended for use as a communal preparation for celebrating the Sacrament of Reconciliation individually at a later date.

An RE teacher and I adapted this liturgy for a class of eight- to nine-year-olds in a Catholic Primary School. The children had already celebrated their First Reconciliation and this liturgy was in preparation for the Feast of Pentecost.

The opening rite and liturgy of the word took place in one corner of the large school hall. The children's lectionary was placed on a book-stand on a table draped with a coloured cloth. There was a lighted candle as well as some flowers and nearby a display stand for the posters.

The class of children sat facing the table and were assisted and supported in their celebration by some of their teachers and parents, as well as several older children. The teacher led the music, a parent read the Gospel passage and I was the liturgy leader.

Following the dialogue using the posters, everyone was sent – a few at a time – to sit round the enormous paperchain ring. The children had made this beforehand and it took up most of the remaining floor space in the hall. Everyone sat facing the large link of the chain bearing their own name.

As the liturgy leader, I then used the following dialogue with the children.

Leader: Jesus asks us to love God and love others like he did, but what can go wrong? What do people sometimes do that spoils the circle of love – the way of living and loving like Jesus?

We will now sit very quietly and ask Jesus in our hearts to help us see the ways in which we have spoilt the circle of love. (About a minute's silence is observed.)

I expect that each of us here has thought of one way in which we have spoilt the circle of love; one way in which we have not loved others as Jesus loves us. So, now let us gently tear the link of the chain that has our own name on it. Look! The circle is damaged – our lack of love spoils the way Jesus wants us to live.

How can things be put right? (I then asked that we each tell Jesus in our hearts that we are really sorry for the times we have not loved as we should and then I led everyone in praying a prayer of sorrow together (see page 105). Then I continued as follows.)

When we tell Jesus we are sorry, does he forgive us? (Yes.)

Let us sit quietly in our places, praying to Jesus, asking him to help us try to live in love from now on.

While gentle music is played, the older children will come round. Please give them your broken link and they will give you a new link made from gold paper. Then wait for one of the grown-ups to come round to staple your link in place, so that, together, we can remake the chain.

(When the paper chain has been remade.) Look at our new circle. Do you think that it looks better than the old one? (Yes.)

When we turn to Jesus in sorrow and ask him to make things right, he makes things even better than they were before – he helps us to grow in love. When we helped to remake the circle, it's a sign that we want to share the love of Jesus with everyone. It's easy to staple pieces of paper, but it's much harder to really live in love. Let us spend a few moments thinking of ways in which we are going to try to live more like Jesus from now on. (Pause for personal reflection.)

Now let us each hold on to our new gold link in the chain and pray

---

Commentary

This penitential service has no absolution or penance. What it does have is an opportunity to reflect communaly on our need for forgiveness and express our sorrow and desire to live in love. The paper chain representing the circle of love – the perfect love we are called to have for each other by Jesus – is something that the children find helpful. It not only shows how our lack of love can spoil things, but also how Jesus can put things right when we turn to him in sorrow and trust.

together the Our Father as a sign that we want to live as the family of God, living and loving in the way that Jesus showed us.

The liturgy ended with a concluding song.

An Advent Family Reconciliation liturgy

This liturgy was devised as a daytime celebration for one Saturday during Advent for families, especially those with children who had

---

Resources

- A children's lectionary, with the Annunciation Gospel reading marked.
- A lay person as reader.
- Two children, in costume, to mime the roles of Mary and Angel Gabriel as the Gospel is read.
- Service sheets, so that everyone can follow and join in.
- A musician or music group would be ideal, but, if necessary, the singing can be led without accompaniment.
- A cassette or CD of gentle music, to be played during the time of individual ministry.
- A tray with containers of lead pencils, colouring pencils, a few erasers and sharpeners.
- A basket of A6-sized prayer cards for those children who have made their First Holy Communion, as well as A5-sized cards depicting a stained-glass window of the nativity, for all the children.
- A large poster of a stained-glass window, if the church doesn't have any such windows that can be easily seen by the children.
- A candle rack, or sand table, with sufficient tea lights for each family to light one, plus tapers and matches.

---

made their First Holy Communion. It was well advertised through-out the parish and local Catholic schools and everyone, whatever their age, was invited.

The actors rehearsed their mime beforehand with the reader. They and the reader were seated at the side of the sanctuary before the liturgy began. The other children sat with their families at the begin-ning of the liturgy.

Sufficient priests were present to cater for the number of people expected, and pairs of chairs were placed around the church for priests and penitents.

A good idea would be to use Bernadette Farrell's 'Litany of the Word' as a gathering song. The responses – 'Alleluia' and 'Maranatha' – are easy for young children to join in.

Opening song

The first three verses of 'The Angel Gabriel', *Laudate*, 113, would be most appropriate.

Welcome and introduction

The priest presider welcomes everyone and explains that the liturgy has been prepared so that the children can play a special role in it. He also introduces the priests, if they are not known to the assembly.

Opening prayer

Priest presider: God our Father,
you sent the Angel Gabriel to ask Mary to be the mother of your Son, Jesus. Mary was so completely open to your word that she said 'Yes'. Help us to open our hearts now to your word and, with trust

in your promises, ask for the Spirit's gift of forgiveness and healing, through Jesus Christ, our Lord.

Response: Amen

Gospel acclamation

See page 27 for suggestions.

Gospel reading

(Everyone is invited to sit for the Gospel reading (Luke 1:26–38), so that the mime can be seen. It may be appropriate to invite the children to come and sit at the front. As the reader reads the Gospel, the actors prayerfully mime what is being described.)

Reader: A reading from the holy Gospel according to Luke.

God sent the angel Gabriel to the town of Nazareth in Galilee with a message for a virgin named Mary. She was engaged to Joseph from the family of King David. The angel greeted Mary and said, 'You are truly blessed! The Lord is with you.' Mary was confused by the angel's words and wondered what they meant. Then the angel told Mary, 'Don't be afraid! God is pleased with you, and you will have a son. His name will be Jesus. He will be great and will be called the Son of God Most High. The Lord God will make him king, as his ancestor David was. He will rule the people of Israel forever, and his kingdom will never end.'

Mary asked the angel, 'How can this happen? I am not married!'

The angel answered, 'The Holy Spirit will come down to you, and God's power will come over you. So your child will be called the holy Son of God.

'Your relative Elizabeth is also going to have a son, even though she is old. No one thought she could ever have a baby, but in three months she will have a son. Nothing is impossible for God!' Mary said, 'I am the Lord's servant! Let it happen as you have said.'

And the angel left her.

This is the Gospel of the Lord.

Dialogue

This may be led by one of the priests, a catechist or liturgy leader, but preferably by someone who is familiar to the children.

Leader: Who did God send to Mary as a special messenger? What was God's message for Mary? What did God want Mary to do? What was Mary's answer? Did she agree to become the mother of Jesus? Why do you think God chose Mary? Was there something special about her?

Yes, Mary was very special because she always did what God wanted her to do. She could have said no to the angel, but she said yes. Mary might have thought that it would be a difficult life being the mother of the Saviour, Jesus, but she said yes to God nonetheless because she loved God so much.

(Now is the time to point to the stained-glass windows or poster of such windows.) Look at the lovely stained-glass windows. Tell me some of the colours that you can see.

What is shining through the windows to let us see the colours? If the day was dull and grey or it was dark outside, could we still see the lovely colours? No. The window needs the light of the sun to shine so that its colours will show up.

In a way, each of us is like a stained-glass window. When we were baptized, we received the light of God's love in our hearts and God wants us to live in such a way that the light of his love can shine out of us and be seen by other people.

Mary is the best example of someone who let the light of God's love shine out of her. She lived perfectly in God's way. We, perhaps, do not always show God's love to others in the best way. Sometimes, perhaps, we do not love as Jesus loves. We are rather like a stained-glass window that has lost its bright colours.

Children, let's think of a few examples of what it means for us to say yes to God as Mary did. Suppose you are playing at home and your mummy or daddy asks you to come and help them to do something, such as help to set the table for dinner or help to clear up some toys. What would be the best answer to give? What should you do so that the light of God's love can shine brightly in you?

Suppose a new child comes to join your class at school. This child has just moved house with his or her family. How do you think that new boy or girl would feel? What would that new boy or girl hope that you would do?

Perhaps you would rather carry on talking to your friends, but, if you take the time to talk to that new child and welcome him or her into your group of friends, help him or her to find where things are around the school, then you will be showing the light of God's love to everyone around you.

Let us all – grown-ups as well – be very still and think for a moment about the times we have lived in a way to let God's light shine brightly in our lives and said yes to what we know God wants us to do. Let us also think about the times when perhaps we have not really said yes to God.

Prayer of sorrow

Priest presider: O my God,
thank you for loving me. I am sorry for the times I have not said yes to you as Mary did. I am sorry for not loving others and not loving you in the best way. Help me to live and love like Jesus.

Response: Amen

Invitation

The priest presider indicates where each priest will be to offer individual ministry.

Priest presider: Those who wish, are invited to approach one of the priests for individual confession and absolution or for a prayer of healing, a word of encouragement and a blessing. The young children are invited to go to the liturgy leaders (he points to the part of the church where they are) where they will be able to colour in stained-glass window pictures. Children who are going to confession are also encouraged to go to the liturgy leaders first to fill in a prayer card. During this time, gentle music will be played. Please pray for each other while you are waiting to see a priest.

(At the end of the individual confessions, the priest presider invites each family, couple or individual to come forward to light a candle as a sign of their prayer, to grow in forgiveness, peace and love. Then the assembly is led in praying the Our Father and in offering a sign of peace.)

Prayer of thanksgiving

Priest presider: Father,
we thank you for sending Jesus to show us how to love. Thank you for your gifts of forgiveness and healing, given to us through the power of the Holy Spirit. Help us in the coming days to open our hearts to welcome the light and love of Jesus more fully into our lives. We ask this through Jesus Christ, our Lord.

Response: Amen

Concluding song

See page 100 for suggestions.

God sent Mary a messenger.
The Angel Gabriel greeted Mary
and said to her, 'You are truly blessed!
The Lord is with you.'

Mary said YES to God.
She said, 'I am the Lord's servant!
Let it happen as you have said.'

Dear God, I want to say YES to you always.
I want the light and love of Jesus
to shine brightly through me.

There are some ways I need to change:

_____

_____

_____

_____

Please give me your forgiveness
and help me to grow in love.
Amen

The wording for the prayer card is given above. On the reverse side, a clip art picture of the Annunciation could be printed, so that the children can colour it in after they have been to confession and prayed silently.

Commentary

This type of celebration helps children who have celebrated First Reconciliation, and their parents, to grow in their use and appreciation of this often neglected sacrament. The mime and dialogue help young children to participate and the involvement of liturgy leaders, helping the little ones to decorate their stained-glass window pictures, frees the parents so that they can seek individual ministry from a priest, whether they are Catholic or not.

The prayer card given to the children who wish to go to confess to a priest is devised in such a way that it simplifies their way of talking to the priest, if they need to. In fact, I have often known children simply show their prayer cards to the priest, who then helps them to talk about what they have written.

There are several photocopyable nativity stained-glass window designs by Clemens Schmidt in *Clip Art for the Liturgical Year* published by The Liturgical Press.

13

Questions people ask

Why take the children aside for a separate liturgy of the word?

Today, children are growing up in a world that can hardly be described as conducive to their spiritual welfare and parents can make light of the obligations they assumed at the baptism of their children, which are to give them a Christian upbringing (DMC, 1). So, it is more important than ever that the whole Christian community helps its children by providing the means whereby they can fulfil their duty of worship and encounter Christ through liturgy.

Children are as important as adults in this regard, as Jesus himself showed. In the midst of his disciples, who, on at least one occasion, had wanted to send the children away (Matthew 19:14), Jesus 'took a little child whom he set by his side and then he said to them, "Anyone who welcomes this little child in my name, welcomes me; and anyone who welcomes me, welcomes the one who sent me"' (Luke 9:47b–48). What stronger affirmation of the place of children in the assembly could anyone possibly demand?

It is not necessary for children to understand everything that is going on in the Mass. Indeed, who can ever completely comprehend the mystery of the Eucharist? However, we may fear for their spiritual harm (DMC, 2) unless the children can have a sense of belonging and be able to participate knowingly, actively and fruitfully and experience the love of God at work in their lives, which we celebrate in liturgy. John J. O'Brien reminds us of what the DMC so rightly asserts:

> that children are capable of celebrating Eucharist. This is especially true when the words and signs of the liturgy are adapted. This

does not mean that liturgy is trivialized or childish in its celebration. What it does mean is that pastoral care and liturgical action draw out children in their openness to mystery, the numinous and the mystical as well as the incarnational stories and images of God found in the Bible.

NDSW, p. 185

Taking children aside for their own liturgy emphasizes their importance, fosters their sense of belonging and helps them to hear God's word and respond to it.

How often should we have a separate liturgy of the word for children?

The DMC does not suggest that there should be a separate liturgy of the word for children every Sunday. In fact, it proposes that *sometimes* this should be arranged (DMC, 17).

Clearly there are occasions during the liturgical year when it is important that the whole assembly should be together for the liturgy. Masses during which the First Holy Communion children celebrate aspects of their preparation, such as thanking God for the gift of creation and Masses during which a baby is baptized, would be occasions when children benefit by remaining within the assembly.

Quality, not quantity, should be an important consideration. It is better to have a well-prepared celebration every two or three weeks than something that is hurriedly put together most weeks. Consideration of the appropriateness, availability of the liturgy team members and adequate time for preparation should be the deciding factors.

Why not let the parents take the children to the liturgy room before Mass begins?

In parishes where a crèche is organized, before Mass begins, the children are taken by their parents to the room where the childminders await them. In most cases, the children remain in the crèche until their parents collect them after Mass. However, the activities described in this book are not those of a crèche but of a liturgy and, in the *Guidelines*, we are reminded that 'to emphasize the unity of the whole assembly the children gather in the church with their families for the introductory rites of the Mass' (see 'Commentary' section of *Guidelines*). In practical terms, if the children were to be taken to the liturgy room before Mass began, when the children processed back into church, they might not know where their families were sitting.

Why have separate age groups?

Separate age groups are recommended so that the language of the dialogue and the images used can be tailored to the level of under-standing and everyday experiences of the children in the group.

What can we do if our parish does not have enough space available?

Where only one room is available for children's liturgy, it may be possible to take a different age group of children on different Sundays. However, it is more likely that a decision would be made about which age group was most in need of having their own sepa-rate liturgy and ideas shared with the priest presider as to how to include the remaining children in the Mass (see Chapter 11).

Do you have to bring the children back at the offertory?

The DMC gives permission for the children to celebrate their own liturgy of the word and rejoin the assembly for the Eucharist, so, yes, the children should be brought back to take part in the procession of the gifts. It has been known for liturgy leaders to organize banner making during children's liturgy of the word, so they do not return until the banner has been completed, which could be any time during the Liturgy of the Eucharist. This, though, is bad practice. In such cases, the children's liturgy seems to have become an end in itself, whereas it is a part of the act of worship of the assembly. (See Chapter 7, where the responses of the children are summarized in a poster.)

Can we be commissioned in the same way as eucharistic ministers are?

At present, the bishops have not authorized any particular form of rite of commissioning for ministers of children's liturgy. Following a training programme for liturgy leaders and helpers in a parish, we devised a form of commissioning that took place during a Family Mass one Sunday. Below is this unofficial text in case your parish or deanery wishes to seek permission from the diocese to use it either during Mass or a liturgy of the word for the community.

A rite of commissioning ministers of children's liturgy

In the homily, the celebrant first explains the reason for this ministry and then presents the people chosen and trained to serve as ministers of children's liturgy in the parish using these or similar words.

Priest: Dear friends in Christ,
our brothers and sisters, N. and N., are to be entrusted with leading and helping the children of our parish community in their own separate liturgies of the word. (The priest pauses and then addresses the candidates.)

In this ministry, you must be examples of Christian living in faith and conduct. You must strive to grow in holiness by pondering on the word of God and striving to live according to the Gospel of Christ. As ministers of the liturgy of the word for children, be especially observant of the Lord's command: 'Love one another as I have loved you.'

(After the address, the candidates stand before the priest, who asks them the following questions.) Are you resolved to undertake the office of ministering to our children by celebrating the liturgy of the word and so building up the Church?

Response: I am.

Priest: Are you resolved to prepare the liturgies with prayerful reflection and celebrate them with loving care?

Response: I am.

(All stand. The candidates kneel and the priest invites the faithful to pray as follows.)

Priest: Dear friends in Christ,
let us pray with confidence to the Father. Let us ask him to bestow his blessings on our brothers and sisters, chosen to be ministers of the liturgy of the word for children. (Pause for silent prayer, then the priest continues.)

Everlasting God, when he read in the synagogue at Nazareth, your Son proclaimed the good news of salvation for which he would give up his life.

Bless ✠ these ministers of the liturgy of the word for children. As they proclaim your words of life to the children of our parish, strengthen their faith that they may proclaim and celebrate your word with conviction and boldness and put into practice what they proclaim. We ask this through Christ our Lord.

Response: Amen

14

Conclusion

When parents bring their child to be baptized, the priest asks them whether or not they clearly understand the responsibility they are accepting, which is 'to train their child in the practice of the faith and to bring him or her up to keep God's commandments as Christ taught us, by loving God and our neighbour'. The child's godparents then declare their willingness to help the child's parents in this task. Whenever the baptism of a child is celebrated during Mass, the role of the whole community in supporting and helping those Christian parents is frequently emphasized by the priest, for we each have a responsibility to help each other grow in faith.

Good liturgy touches our lives in such a way that we are renewed in our mission as Christians. In liturgy the divine action is communicated to us through human gestures, words and symbols, so the first task of parents in helping their children to understand the basic liturgical gestures and concepts of the Mass is to teach their children the meaning of ordinary gestures and signs that people use among themselves. By experiencing the meaning of welcoming, exchanging greetings, forgiving and saying sorry, listening, thanking and sharing, as well as taking part in special family meals and celebrations, children can be trained for worship. Above all, parents need to give their children the experience of daily prayer and the opportunity to take part in Mass along with the family (DMC, 10).

Liturgy has an educative value of its own, even for children, but formal catechesis is also required and this needs to include an understanding of the Mass (DMC, 12). Catechesis forms in faith, liturgy celebrates faith. It is important for Christian parents and educators to keep the distinction between liturgy and catechesis in mind. Confusing these activities weakens liturgy by diverting us from its true purpose (CAC, p. 69). Liturgical formation (see Glossary) is important for everyone and the efforts of the worshipping community to celebrate Mass appropriately with children are doomed to failure unless we give great attention to the liturgical formation of children and regard it as an essential prerequisite for their participation in liturgy, particularly in the Mass.

The parish community has a vital role to play in helping all the children to grow in their understanding of liturgy and develop their ability to participate in worship. Genuine collaboration of priests and people and creativity in liturgy are needed to engender a real sense of reverence, awe and celebration, by which we each allow the ritual to engage our whole being. Paul Philibert describes what many of us may, sadly, have discovered from our own experience of poor liturgy:

> Liturgy fails when the Gospel stories are simply perceived as repeated familiar tales, heard year after year, with the flatness of yesterday's newspaper. Liturgy succeeds only when the Gospel stories are recognized as treasures of life-giving pre-understandings which connect us in imagination and desire with the promises of God's kingdom preached by Jesus.
>
> AFW, pp. 71–2

Good liturgy builds faith, bad liturgy weakens faith. Liturgy is something to be done, not something to be read. When we consider how much care is needed to prepare and celebrate good liturgy with children, what does that tell us about the importance of careful preparation and prayerful celebration for every liturgy? Good liturgy is that which enables each of us to experience the power of ritual to form and transform us, as Gertrud Mueller Nelson describes:

> In sacramental action, the bread is broken, shared and consumed. The precious incense is burned away . . . But each of these ordinary and natural things has engaged us physically and emotionally in a truth about the mysteries of our human nature and the story of our salvation. Each serves a purpose: to hold, for a time, a

meaning and to point beyond itself to mystery . . . Ritual is the formal and physical expression of what is holy.

CAC, p. 55

Formation in good practice is particularly important for those who plan children's liturgy, yet, even with all the training and planning, we must not forget the importance of prayer and the role of the Spirit. As Joan Patano Vos assures us:

a perfect celebration is not one in which everything goes as planned (such a liturgy exists only in heaven), but one in which the participants have known God's gift of self to us and made Christ's prayer of praise and thanksgiving their own.

CAC, p. 97

From my experience of celebrating liturgy with children, including those with learning difficulties, in schools and parishes, I have found the provisions for adaptation of the liturgy in the DMC to be adequate for the spiritual needs of children and the whole liturgical assembly, though these directives are not always appropriately followed!

How many times have we heard anguished cries about children who have stopped going to church? Any return, to be meaningful, has to be a *free* return, a return where the individual can see the value of the Church community. I believe that good experiences of liturgy in childhood and adolescence will certainly facilitate a *free* return. Without the confidence and maturity gained through liturgical formation, we risk failing our children and young people, who rightly look to the whole Christian community to nurture their growth in faith. For, as two Lasalian Brothers – Gerard Rummery and Damian Lundy – with wide experience in Christian formation wrote:

I do not believe alone. 'WE believe.' I am baptized into the faith of the community, and as I grow I look to my fellow Christians to be accepted, nourished, forgiven, healed, blessed, renewed, challenged and enlightened, so that I in my turn, with my brothers and sisters, may become the good news which will save the world.

GIF, p. 4

Appendix 1

Directory for Masses with Children

Introduction

1 The Church must show special concern for baptized children who have yet to be fully initiated through the sacraments of confirmation and eucharist as well as for children who have only recently been admitted to holy communion. The circumstances of contemporary life in which children grow up are less favorable to their spiritual progress.[1] In addition parents sometimes scarcely fulfill the obligations they accepted at the baptism of their children to bring them up as Christians.

2 In the upbringing of children in the Church a special difficulty arises from the fact that liturgical celebrations, especially the eucharist, cannot fully exercise their inherent pedagogical force upon children.[2] Although the vernacular may now be used at Mass, still the words and signs have not been sufficiently adapted to the capacity of children.

In fact, even in daily life children do not always understand all their experiences with adults but rather may find them boring. It cannot therefore be expected of the liturgy that everything must always be intelligible to them. Nonetheless there is a fear of spiritual harm if over the years children repeatedly experience in the Church things that are barely comprehensible; for recent psychological study has established how profoundly children are formed by the religious experience of infancy and early childhood, because of the special religious receptivity proper to those years.[3]

3 The Church follows its Master, who 'put his arms around the little children . . . and blessed them' (Mark 10:16). It cannot leave children in the condition described. The Second Vatican Council had already spoken in the Constitution on the Liturgy about the need of liturgical adaptation for various groups.[4] Soon afterward, especially in the first Synod of Bishops held in Rome in 1967, the Church began to consider more carefully how participation by children could be facilitated. On the occasion of the Synod, the President of the Consilium for the Implementation of the Constitution on the Liturgy said explicitly that it could not be a matter of 'creating some entirely special rite but rather of retaining, shortening, or omitting some elements or of making a more appropriate selection of texts.'[5]

4 All the details of eucharistic celebration with a congregation were determined in the General Instruction of the revised Roman Missal published in 1969. Then this Congregation began to prepare a special Directory for Masses with Children, as a supplement to the Instruction. This was done in response to repeated petitions from the entire Catholic world and with the cooperation of men and women specialists from almost every nation.

5 Like the General Instruction, this Directory reserves some adaptations to the conferences of bishops or to individual bishops.[6]

Adaptations of the Mass for children may be necessary in a given country but cannot be included in a general directory. In accord with the Constitution on the Liturgy, art. 40, the same conferences of bishops are to propose such adaptations to the Apostolic See for introduction into the liturgy with its consent.

6 The Directory is concerned with children who have not yet entered the period of preadolescence. It does not speak directly of children who are physically or mentally handicapped, because a broader adaptation is sometimes necessary for them.[7] Nevertheless, the following norms may also be applied to the handicapped, with the necessary changes.

7 The first chapter of the Directory (nos. 8–15) gives a kind of foundation by considering the variety of ways in which children are introduced to the eucharistic liturgy. The second chapter (nos. 16–19) briefly treats Masses with adults in which children also take part. Finally, the third chapter (nos. 20–54) treats at greater length Masses with children in which only some adults take part.

Chapter one
The introduction of children to the eucharistic celebration

8 A fully Christian life is inconceivable without participation in the liturgical services in which the faithful, gathered into a single assembly, celebrate the paschal mystery. Therefore, the religious initiation of children must be in harmony with this purpose.[8] The Church baptizes children and therefore, relying on the gifts conferred by this sacrament, it must be concerned that once baptized they grow in communion with Christ and each other. The sign and pledge of that communion is participation in the eucharistic table, for which children are being prepared or led to a deeper realization of its meaning. This liturgical and eucharistic formation may not be separated from their general education, both human and Christian; indeed it would be harmful if their liturgical formation lacked such a foundation.

9 For this reason all who have a part in the formation of children should work together and consult toward one objective: that, even if children already have some feeling for God and the things of God, they may also experience in proportion to their age and personal development the human values that are present in the eucharistic celebration. These values include the community activity, exchange of greetings, capacity to listen and to seek and grant pardon, expression of gratitude, experience of symbolic actions, a meal of friendship, and festive celebration.[9]

Eucharistic catechesis, dealt with in no. 12, should develop such human values. Then, depending on their age and their psychological and social situation, children will gradually open their minds to the perception of Christian values and the celebration of the mystery of Christ.[10]

10 The Christian family has the greatest role in instilling these human and Christian values.[11] Thus Christian formation, provided by parents and other educators, should be strongly encouraged in relation to the liturgical formation of children as well.

By reason of the duty in conscience freely accepted at the baptism of their children, parents have an obligation to teach them gradually how to pray. This they do by praying with them each day and by introducing them to prayers said privately.[12] If children, prepared in this way even from their early years, take part in the Mass with their family whenever they wish, they will easily begin to sing and to pray in the liturgical community and indeed will already have some initial idea of the eucharistic mystery.

If, however, the parents are weak in faith but still wish their children to receive Christian formation, they should be urged at least to communicate to their children the human values mentioned already and, when the occasion arises, to participate in meetings of parents and in non-eucharistic celebrations held with children.

11 In addition, the Christian communities to which the individual families belong or in which the children live also have a responsibility toward children baptized in the Church. By giving witness to the gospel, living communal charity, and actively celebrating the mysteries of Christ, the Christian community is an excellent school of Christian and liturgical formation for the children who live in it.

Within the Christian community, godparents or other persons noted for their dedicated service can, out of apostolic zeal, contribute greatly to the necessary catechesis in the case of families that fail in their obligation toward the children's Christian upbringing.

Preschool programs, Catholic schools, and various kinds of associations for children serve these same needs in a special way.

12 Even in the case of children, the liturgy itself always exerts its own inherent power to instruct.[13] Yet within religious-education

programs in the schools and parishes the necessary importance should be given to catechesis on the Mass.[14] This catechesis should be directed to the child's active, conscious, and authentic participation.[15] 'Suited to children's age and capabilities, it should, by means of the main rites and prayers of the Mass, aim at conveying its meaning, including what relates to taking part in the Church's life.'[16] This is especially true of the text of the eucharistic prayer and of the acclamations by which the children take part in this prayer.

The catechesis preparing children for first communion calls for special mention. In it they should learn not only the truths of faith regarding the eucharist but also how from first communion on – after being prepared according to their capacity by penance – they can as fully integrated members of Christ's Body take part actively with the people of God in the eucharist, sharing in the Lord's table and the community of their brothers and sisters.

13 Various kinds of celebrations may also play a major role in the liturgical formation of children and in their preparation for the Church's liturgical life. By the very fact of such celebrations children easily perceive some liturgical elements, for example, greetings, silence, and common praise (especially when this is sung together). But care must be taken that the instructive element does not become dominant in these celebrations.

14 Depending on the capacity of the children, the word of God should have a greater and greater place in these celebrations. In fact, as the children's spiritual capacity develops, celebrations of the word of God in the strict sense should be held rather frequently, especially during Advent and Lent.[17] These celebrations are able to encourage in the children an appreciation of the word of God.

15 While all that has been said remains true, the final purpose of all liturgical and eucharistic formation must always be a greater and greater conformity to the gospel in the daily life of the children.

Chapter two
Masses with adults in which children also participate

16 In many places parish Masses are celebrated, especially on Sundays and feast days, at which a good many children take part along with the large number of adults. At these Masses the witness of adult believers can have a great effect upon the children. Adults can in turn benefit spiritually from experiencing the part that the children have within the Christian community. The Christian spirit of the family is greatly fostered when children take part in these Masses together with their parents and other family members.

Infants who as yet are unable or unwilling to take part in the Mass may be brought in at the end of Mass to be blessed together with the rest of the community. This may be done, for example, if some parish helpers have been taking care of them in a separate area.

17 Nevertheless, in Masses of this kind it is necessary to take great care that the children present do not feel neglected because of their inability to participate or to understand what happens and what is proclaimed in the celebration. Some account should be taken of their presence: for example, by speaking to them directly in the brief comments (as at the beginning and the end of Mass) and at some point in the homily.

Sometimes, moreover, if the place itself and the nature of the individuals permit, it possibly will be appropriate to celebrate the liturgy of the word, including a homily, with the children in a separate, but not too distant, location. Then, before the eucharistic liturgy begins, the children are led to the place where the adults have meanwhile celebrated their own liturgy of the word.

18 In these Masses it may also be very helpful to give some tasks to the children. They may, for example, bring forward the gifts or sing one or other of the songs of the Mass.

19 If the number of children is large, it may at times be suitable to

plan this kind of Mass so that it corresponds more closely to the needs of the children. In this case the homily should be directed to them but in such a way that adults may also benefit from it. Wherever the bishop permits, in addition to the adaptations already provided in the Order of Mass, one or other of the particular adaptations described later in the Directory may be employed in a Mass celebrated with adults in which children also participate.

Chapter three
Masses with children in which only a few adults participate

20 In addition to the Masses in which children take part with their parents and other family members (which are not always possible everywhere), Masses with children primarily in which only a few adults take part are recommended, especially during the week. From the beginning of the liturgical reform it has been clear to everyone that some adaptations are necessary in these Masses.[18]

Such adaptations, but only those of a more general kind, will be considered later (nos. 38–54).

21 It is always necessary to keep in mind that such eucharistic celebrations must lead children toward the celebration of Mass with adults, especially the Masses at which the Christian community must come together on Sundays.[19] Thus, apart from adaptations that are necessary because of the children's age, the result should not be entirely special rites, markedly different from the Order of Mass celebrated with a congregation.[20] The purpose of the various elements should always correspond with what is said in the General Instruction of the Roman Missal on individual points, even if at times for pastoral reasons an absolute *identity* cannot be insisted upon.

Offices and ministries in the celebration

22 The principles of active and conscious participation are in a sense even more significant for Masses celebrated with children. Every effort should therefore be made to increase this participation and to make it more intense. For this reason as many children as possible should have special parts in the celebration: for example, preparing the place and the altar (see no. 29), acting as cantor (see no. 24), singing in a choir, playing musical instruments (see no. 32), proclaiming the readings (see nos. 24 and 47), responding during the homily (see no. 48), reciting the intentions of the general intercessions, bringing the gifts to the altar, and performing similar activities in accord with the usage of various peoples (see no. 34).

To encourage participation, it will also sometimes be helpful to have several additions, for example, the insertion of motives for giving thanks before the priest begins the dialogue of the preface.

In all this, it should be kept in mind that external activities will remain fruitless and even harmful if they do not serve the internal participation of the children. Thus sacred silence has its importance even in Masses with children (see no. 37). These things should be attended to with great care so that the children do not forget that all the forms of participation reach their high point in eucharistic communion, when the body and blood of Christ are received as spiritual nourishment.[21]

23 It is the responsibility of the priest who celebrates a Mass with children to make the celebration festive, familial, and meditative.[22] Even more than in Masses with adults, the priest should bring about this kind of attitude of mind which depends on his personal preparation and his manner of acting and speaking with others.

The priest should be concerned above all about the dignity, clarity, and simplicity of his actions and gestures. In speaking to the children he should express himself so that he will be easily understood, while avoiding any childish style of speech.

The free use of introductory comments[23] will lead children to a genuine liturgical participation, but these should not be merely didactic explanations.

It will help him to reach the hearts of the children if the priest sometimes expresses the invitations in his own words, for example, at the penitential rite, the prayer over the gifts, the Lord's Prayer, the sign of peace, and communion.

24 Since the eucharist is always the action of the entire ecclesial community, the participation of at least some adults is desirable. These should be present not as monitors but as people who by praying with the children are participating in the Mass and who can help them to the extent necessary.

With the consent of the pastor or rector of the church, nothing forbids one of the adults who is participating in a Mass with children from speaking to the children after the gospel reading, especially if the priest finds it difficult to adapt himself to the mentality of children. In this matter the norms issued by the Congregation for the Clergy should be observed.

Even in Masses with children the diversity of ministries should be encouraged so that the Mass may stand out clearly as the celebration of a community.[24] For example, readers and cantors, whether children or adults, should be employed. In this way a variety of voices will keep the children from becoming bored.

Place and time of celebration

25 The primary place for the eucharistic celebration for children is the church. Within the church, however, a space should be carefully chosen, if available, that will be suited to the number of participants. It should be a place where the children can act freely according to the requirements of a living liturgy that is suited to their age.

If, however, the church does not satisfy these demands, it will sometimes be suitable to celebrate the eucharist with children outside a place of worship. But in that case the location chosen should be appropriate and worthy of such a celebration.[25]

26 For Masses with children the time of day should be chosen that best corresponds to the circumstances of their lives so that they may be most open to hearing the word of God and to celebrating the eucharist.

27 Weekday Mass in which children participate can certainly be celebrated with greater effect and less danger of boredom if it does not take place every day (for example, in boarding schools). Moreover, preparation can be more careful if there is a longer interval between diverse celebrations.

Sometimes it will be preferable to have common prayer, to which the children may also contribute spontaneously, or else a common meditation, or a celebration of the word of God. These are ways of continuing the eucharistic celebrations already held and of fostering a deeper participation in subsequent celebrations.

28 When the number of children who celebrate the eucharist together is very great, attentive and conscious participation becomes more difficult. Therefore, if possible, several groups should be formed; these should not be set up rigidly according to age but with regard for the children's progress in religious formation and catechetical preparation.

During the week such groups appropriately may be invited to the sacrifice of the Mass on different days.

Preparation for the celebration

29 Each eucharistic celebration with children should be carefully prepared beforehand, especially with regard to the prayers, songs, readings, and intentions of the general intercessions. This should be done in discussion with the adults and with the children who will have a special ministry in these Masses. If possible, some of the children should take part in preparing and ornamenting the place of celebration and preparing the cup with the plate and the cruets. Presupposing the appropriate internal participation, such activity may also help to develop the spirit of community celebration.

Singing and music

30 Since singing must be given great importance in all celebrations, it is to be especially encouraged in every way for Masses celebrated with children, in view of their special affinity for music.[26] The culture of various peoples and the children's own capabilities should be taken into account.

   If possible, the acclamations should be sung by the children rather than recited, especially the acclamations that form part of the eucharistic prayer.

31 To facilitate the children's participation in singing the *Gloria, Credo, Sanctus,* and the *Agnus Dei,* it is permitted to use with the melodies appropriate vernacular texts, accepted by competent authority, even if these do not correspond exactly to the liturgical texts.[27]

32 The use of 'musical instruments can also add a great deal' in Masses with children, especially if they are played by the children themselves.[28] The playing of instruments will help to sustain the singing or to encourage the reflection of the children; sometimes in their own fashion instruments express festive joy and the praise of God.

   Special care should always be taken, however, that the musical accompaniment does not overpower the singing or become a distraction rather than a help to the children. Music should correspond to the purpose intended for the different times at which it is played during the Mass.

   With these precautions and with due need and special discretion, recorded music may also be used in Masses with children, in accord with norms established by the conferences of bishops.

Gestures

33 In view of the nature of the liturgy as an activity of the entire person and in view of the psychology of children, participation by

means of gestures and posture should be strongly encouraged in Masses with children, with due regard for age and local customs. Much depends not only on the gestures of the priest,[29] but also on the manner in which the children conduct themselves as a community.

If, in accord with the norm of the General Instruction of the Roman Missal,[30] a conference of bishops adapts the gestures and postures at Mass to the mentality of a people, it should take the special condition of children into account or should decide on certain adaptations that are for children only.

34 Among the actions that are considered under this heading, processions and other activities that involve physical participation deserve special mention.

The children's entering in procession with the priest celebrant serves to help them better to experience a sense of the communion that is thus being created.[31] The participation of at least some children in the procession with the Book of Gospels makes clearer the presence of Christ announcing the word to his people. The procession of children with the cup and the gifts expresses more clearly the value and meaning of the preparation of the gifts. The communion procession, if properly arranged, helps greatly to develop the children's devotion.

Visual elements

35 The liturgy of the Mass itself contains many visual elements and these should be given great prominence with children. This is especially true of the particular visual elements in the course of the liturgical year, for example, the veneration of the cross, the Easter candle, the lights on the feast of the Presentation of the Lord, and the variety of colors and liturgical appointments.

In addition to these visual elements that belong to the celebration itself and to the place of celebration, it is appropriate to introduce other related elements that will permit children to perceive visually the wonderful works that God performed in creation and redemption and thus support their prayer. The liturgy should never appear as something dry and merely intellectual.

36 For the same reason, the use of pictures prepared by the children themselves may be useful, for example, as illustrations of a homily, as visual expressions of the intentions of the general intercessions, or as inspirations to reflection.

Silence

37 Even in Masses with children 'silence should be observed at the designated times as part of the celebration'[32] lest too great a place be given to external action. In their own way children are also genuinely capable of reflection. They need some guidance, however, so that they will learn how, in keeping with the different moments of the Mass (for example, after communion or even after the homily[33]), to recollect themselves, meditate briefly, or praise and pray to God in their hearts.[34]

Besides this, care should be taken, much more than in Masses with adults, that the liturgical texts should be proclaimed unhurriedly and intelligibly, with the necessary pauses.

Parts of the Mass

38 The general structure of the Mass, which 'is made up as it were of two parts: the liturgy of the word and the liturgy of the eucharist', should always be maintained, as should certain rites to open and conclude the celebration.[35] Within individual parts of the celebration, the adaptations that follow seem necessary if children are truly to experience, in their own way and according to the psychological patterns of childhood, 'the mystery of faith . . . by means of rites and prayers.'[36]

39 Some rites and texts should never be adapted for children lest the difference between Masses with children and the Masses with adults

become too pronounced.[37] These are 'the acclamations and the responses of the faithful to the priest's greeting',[38] the Lord's Prayer, and the Trinitarian formulary at the end of the blessing with which the priest concludes the Mass. It is urged, moreover, that children should become accustomed to the Nicene Creed little by little, the right to use the Apostles' Creed indicated in no. 49 remaining intact.

A. *Introductory rite*

40 The introductory rite of Mass has as its purpose 'that the faithful coming together take on the form of a community and prepare themselves to listen properly to God's word and to celebrate the eucharist worthily.'[39] Therefore every effort should be made to create this disposition in the children and not to jeopardize it by any excess of rites which are set forth here.

It is sometimes permissible to omit one or other element of the introductory rite or perhaps to expand another element. There should always be at least some introductory element, which is completed by the opening prayer. In choosing individual elements, care should be taken that each one be used from time to time and that none be entirely neglected.

B. *Reading and explanation of the word of God*

41 Since readings taken from Sacred Scripture 'form the main part of the liturgy of the word',[40] even in Masses celebrated with children biblical reading should never be omitted.

42 With regard to the number of readings on Sundays and feast days, the decrees of the conferences of bishops are to be observed. If three or even two readings appointed on Sundays or weekdays can be understood by children only with difficulty, it is permissible to read two or only one of them, but the gospel reading should never be omitted.

43 If all the readings assigned to the day seem to be unsuited to the capacity of the children, it is permissible to choose readings or a

reading either from the Lectionary for Mass or directly from the Bible, but taking into account the liturgical seasons. It is recommended, moreover, that the individual conferences of bishops see to the composition of lectionaries for Masses with children.

If, because of the limited capacity of the children, it seems necessary to omit one or other verse of a biblical reading, this should be done cautiously and in such a way 'that the meaning of the text or the intent and, as it were, style of the Scriptures are not distorted.'[41]

44 In the choice of readings the criterion to be followed is the quality rather than the quantity of the texts from Sacred Scripture. A shorter reading is not in itself always more suited to children than a lengthy reading. Everything depends on the spiritual advantage that the reading can bring to the children.

45 In the biblical texts 'God is speaking to his people ... (and) Christ is present in the midst of the faithful through his own word.'[42] Paraphrases of Sacred Scripture should therefore be avoided. On the other hand, the use of translations that may already exist for the catechesis of children and that are accepted by the competent authority is recommended.

46 Verses of psalms, carefully selected in accord with the understanding of children, or a song in the form of psalmody or the *Alleluia* with a simple verse should be sung between the readings. The children should always have a part in this singing, but sometimes a reflective silence may be substituted for the singing.

If only a single reading is chosen, the singing may follow the homily.

47 All the elements that will help explain the readings should be given great consideration so that the children may make the biblical readings their own and may come more and more to appreciate better the value of God's word.

Among such elements are the introductory comments that may precede the readings[43] and that by explaining the context or by introducing the text itself help the children to listen better and more fruitfully. The interpretation and illustration of the readings from Sacred Scripture in the Mass on a saint's day may include an account of the saint's life, not only in the homily but even before the biblical readings in the form of an introduction.

Depending on the text of the reading, it may be helpful for the children to read it in parts distributed among them, as is provided for the reading of the Lord's passion during Holy Week.

48 The homily explaining the word of God should be given great prominence in all Masses with children. Sometimes the homily intended for children should become a dialogue with them, unless it is preferred that they should listen in silence.

49 If the profession of faith occurs at the end of the liturgy of the word, the Apostles' Creed may be used with children, especially because it is part of their catechetical formation.

C. Presidential prayers

50 The priest is permitted to choose from the Roman Missal texts of presidential prayers more suited to children, so that he may truly associate the children with himself. But he is to take into account the liturgical season.

51 Since these prayers were composed for adult members of the faithful, however, the principle simply of choosing from among them sometimes does not serve the purpose of having the children regard the prayers as an expression of their own life and religious experience.[44] If this is the case, nothing prevents the text of prayers of the Roman Missal from being adapted to the needs of children, but this should be done in such a way that, preserving the purpose of the prayer and to some extent its substance as well, the priest avoids anything that is foreign to the literary genre of a presidential prayer, such as moral exhortations or a childish manner of speech.

52 The eucharistic prayer is of the greatest importance in the eucharist celebrated with children because it is the high point of the entire celebration.[45] Much depends on the manner in which the priest proclaims this prayer[46] and on the way the children take part by listening and making their acclamations.

The disposition of mind required for this central part of the celebration and the calm and reverence with which everything is done must make the children as attentive as possible. Their attention should be on the real presence of Christ on the altar under the elements of bread and wine, on his offering, on the thanksgiving through him and with him and in him, and on the Church's offering, which is made at that moment and by which the faithful offer themselves and their lives with Christ to the eternal Father in the Holy Spirit.

For the present, the four eucharistic prayers approved by the supreme authority for Masses with adults and introduced into liturgical use are to be employed until the Apostolic See makes other provisions for Masses with children.*

D. Rites before Communion

53 When the eucharistic prayer has ended, the Lord's Prayer, the breaking of bread, and the invitation to communion should always follow,[47] because these elements have the principal significance in the structure of this part of the Mass.

E. Communion and the following rites

54 Everything should be done so that the children who are properly disposed and who have already been admitted to the eucharist may go to the holy table calmly and with recollection and thus take part fully in the eucharistic mystery. If possible, there should be singing, suited to the children, during the communion procession.[48]

The comments that precede the final blessing[49] are important in Masses with children. Before they are dismissed, they need some repetition and application of what they have heard, but this should be done in a very few words. In particular, this is the appropriate time to express the connection between the liturgy and life.

At least sometimes, depending on the liturgical seasons and different occasions in the children's life, the priest should use more expanded forms of blessing, but at the end should always retain the Trinitarian formula with the sign of the cross.[50]

---

55 The contents of the Directory have as their purpose to help children readily and joyfully to encounter Christ together in the eucharistic celebration and to stand with him in the presence of the Father.[51] If they are formed by conscious and active participation in the eucharistic sacrifice and meal, they should learn better day by day, at home and away from home, to proclaim Christ to others among their family and among their peers by living the 'faith, that works through love' (Galatians 5:6).

This Directory was prepared by the Congregation for Divine Worship. On 22 October 1973, Pope Paul VI approved and confirmed it and ordered that it be published.

Congregation for Divine Worship, 1 November 1973, the solemnity of All Saints.

By special mandate of the Supreme Pontiff.

+ Jean Cardinal Villot
Secretary of State

+ Annibale Bugnini
Titular Archbishop of Diocletiana
Secretary of the Congregation for Divine Worship

Notes

1 See Congregation for the Clergy, *General Catechetical Directory* (hereafter, GCD), no. 5: *Acta Apostolicæ Sedis*, Commentarium officiale (Vatican City; hereafter, AAS) 64 (1972), pp. 101–102.

2 See Vatican Council II, Constitution on the Liturgy *Sacrosanctum Concilium*, 4 December 1963 (hereafter, SC), art. 33.

3 See GCD, no. 78: AAS 64 (1972), pp. 146–147.

4 See SC, art. 38; see also Congregation for Divine Worship, Instruction *Actio pastoralis*, on Masses with special groups, 15 May 1969: AAS 61 (1969), pp. 806–811.

5 Consilium for the Implementation of the Constitution on the Liturgy, 'De Liturgia in prima Synodo Episcoporum' (hereafter, 'De Liturgia'), *Notitiæ* 3 (1967), p. 368.

6 See nos. 19, 32, 33 of this Directory.

7 See the Order of Mass with deaf and mute children of German-speaking regions approved, that is, confirmed by this Congregation, 26 June 1970 (Protocol no. 1546/70).

8 See SC, art. 14, 19.

9 See GCD, no. 25: AAS 64 (1972), p. 114.

10 See Vatican Council II, Declaration on Christian Education *Gravissimum educationis*, 28 October 1965 (hereafter, GE), no. 2.

11 See GE, no. 3.

12 See GCD, no. 78: AAS 64 (1972), pp. 146–147.

13 See SC, art. 33.

14 See Congregation of Rites, Instruction *Eucharisticum mysterium*, on worship of the eucharist, 25 May 1967 (hereafter, EuchMyst), no. 14: AAS 59 (1967), p. 550.

15 See GCD, no. 25: AAS 64 (1972), p. 114.

16 See EuchMyst, no. 14: AAS 59 (1967), p. 550; GCD, no. 57: AAS 64 (1972), p. 131.

17 See SC, art. 35:4.

18 See no. 3 of this Directory.

19 See SC, art. 42 and 106.

20 See 'De Liturgia', *Notitiæ* 3 (1967), p. 368.

21 See pages 7–70, General Instruction of the Roman Missal (hereafter, GIRM), no. 56.

22 See no. 37 of this Directory.

23 See GIRM, no. 11.

24 See SC, art. 28.

25 See GIRM, no. 253.

26 See GIRM, no. 19.

27 See Congregation of Rites, Instruction *Musicam sacram*, on music in the liturgy, 5 March 1967 (hereafter, MS), no. 55: AAS 59 (1967), p. 316.

28 See MS, no. 62: AAS 59 (1967), p. 318.

29 See no. 23 of this Directory.

30 See GIRM, no. 21.

31 See GIRM, no. 24.

32 GIRM, no. 23.

33 See EuchMyst, no. 38: AAS 59 (1967), p. 562.

34 See GIRM, no. 23.

35 See GIRM, no. 8.

36 SC, art. 48.

37 See no. 21 of this Directory.

38 GIRM, no. 15.

39 GIRM, no. 24.

40 GIRM, no. 33.

41 The Roman Missal, *Lectionary for Mass*, typical edition, 1969, Introduction, no. 7d; see also 2nd English edition, 1981, Introduction, no. 77.

42 GIRM, no. 33.

43 See GIRM, no. 11.

44 See Consilium for the Implementation of the Constitution on the Liturgy, Instruction *Comme le prévoit*, on the translation of liturgical texts for celebrations with a congregation, 25 January 1969, no. 20.

45 See GIRM, no. 54.

46 See nos. 23 and 37 of this Directory.

* After the promulgation of this Directory, three eucharistic prayers for children were published by the Congregation for Divine Worship on 1 November 1974. These prayers may be used at Masses in which the majority of those present are children, in those countries in which the conference of bishops has approved their use.

47 See no. 23 of this Directory.

48 See MS, no. 32: AAS 59 (1967), p. 309.

49 See GIRM, no. 11.

50 See no. 39 of this Directory.

51 See Order of Mass, Liturgy of the Eucharist, Eucharistic Prayer II.

Appendix 2

Liturgy of the Word with Children
Guidelines

Foreword

This document is intended to encourage all involved in the ministry of the word with children. It may be particularly helpful for priest and people to reflect on it together, sharing their experiences, insights, and any difficulties.

These guidelines for the preparation and celebration of this liturgy may need adapting to local pastoral needs and circumstances. This recommendation is already found in the *Directory for Masses with Children*, an official Roman document produced in 1973 to supplement and adapt the principles for good celebration found in the *General Instruction of the Roman Missal* and in the *Introduction* to the *Lectionary for Mass* (revised 1981). It is strongly recommended that these guidelines be read in conjunction with these important documents on which they depend.

> *[In Masses with adults] it is necessary to take great care that the children present do not feel neglected because of their inability to participate or to understand what happens and what is proclaimed in the celebration. Some account should be taken of their presence: for example, by speaking to them directly in the introductory comments (as in the beginning and the end of Mass) and at some point in the homily.*
>
> *Sometimes, moreover, if the place itself and the nature of the community permit, it will be appropriate to celebrate the liturgy of*

the word, including a homily, with the children in a separate, but not too distant, room. Then, before the eucharistic liturgy begins, the children are led to the place where the adults have meanwhile celebrated their own liturgy of the word.

Directory for Masses with Children (DMC), 17

Introduction

On Sunday the Church comes together to celebrate in word and eucharist the mystery of our Lord's death and resurrection, the paschal mystery. The gathered assembly of the baptised is one of the ways Christ is present: *For where two or three are gathered in my name, I am there among them. (Matthew 18:20)* Our celebration must include everyone: young and old.

In many places, children together with parents and leaders celebrate the liturgy of the word in a separate place. Some parishes have been celebrating like this for a number of years. In other places a liturgy of the word with children is in its infancy or at the planning stage. These guidelines seek to make clear and encourage what is good practice and to affirm and develop the ministries involved in this celebration of God's word.

General principles of liturgy

- Liturgy is the praise and worship of God.
- Liturgy is the source and summit of the Church's life and our lives.
- It is the right and duty of all the baptised, both children and adults.
- The function of liturgy is to build up the members of Christ's body, to strengthen us in preaching Christ.
- Liturgy is action and symbol; it speaks to the whole person, it involves all the senses: sight, touch, sound, taste and smell.

- Participating in liturgy forms our habits because we are ritual people and learn through repetition and copying.

- In liturgy we discover the riches of prayer, through word and gesture, silence and stillness.

- The purpose of adapting liturgy for children is to lead them into full, conscious and active participation in the liturgy of the parish.

- Liturgy with children, as with adults, demands dignity, clarity, and simplicity.

Elements

The liturgy of the word

The liturgy of the word at Mass contains the following elements: readings and chants from scripture, the homily, profession of faith and general intercessions. The word is proclaimed in three readings on Sundays and festivals. The first reading is from the Old Testament (or the Acts of the Apostles in the Easter Season). It is followed by a psalm; itself part of God's word, the psalm also forms the assembly's response to the first reading. The second reading is taken from an apostle, either a letter or from the Book of Revelation. The gospel is greeted in song with an acclamation which often accompanies a procession with the Book of the Gospels. Christ is present in his word.

Throughout Ordinary Time a gospel is read over the course of a year. In Year A: the gospel of Matthew; B: Mark; C: Luke. The gospel of John is read during the seasons of Lent and Easter; it also features part way through the year of Mark.

Each Sunday, the first reading from the Old Testament is chosen to harmonise with the gospel passage. The second reading on the other hand follows one or other letter from the New Testament on its own cycle; it is independent of the gospel and you should not expect to find a link.

During the other seasons of the year (Advent–Christmas, Lent–Easter), there is usually greater harmony between all three readings.

The homily is an integral part of the liturgy. In the context of the season or feast, it develops some point of the biblical readings or of another text of the Mass. It explores the mysteries of faith and the standards of the Christian life. The homily leads people from the liturgy of the word to celebrate the liturgy of the eucharist whole-heartedly so that, nourished by God's word and by the body and blood of Christ, the assembly is strengthened to proclaim Christ in lives renewed.

The profession of faith and the general intercessions are part of the assembly's response to the word of God proclaimed. We call to mind the teachings of our faith before celebrating the mystery of our faith in the Eucharist, and then in common prayer we intercede: for the Church and for the world, for all in need and for the local community.

In celebrating a liturgy of the word with children the structure can be outlined as follows: proclaiming the word, responding to the word, and intercession.

Proclaiming the word

> Since readings taken from holy Scripture 'form the main part of the liturgy of the word' even in Masses celebrated with children biblical reading should never be omitted. (DMC 41)

Books containing the word of God proclaimed in the liturgy remind the hearers of the presence of God speaking to his people. They are signs and symbols of the sacred and so care must be taken to ensure that they are worthy and beautiful. The official introduction to the lectionary for Mass insists that the books from which the word of God is proclaimed must not be replaced with other 'pastoral aids': for instance missalettes, hand missals, or preparation books for leaders.

Three passages from scripture are given in the lectionary for Mass. If they are not suitable to the understanding of children two may be omitted (DMC 42), but the gospel is always proclaimed.

Brief introductory comments may precede a reading in order to help the children appreciate its biblical context, to listen attentively and make the Scripture their own.

Christian communities discover and deepen their faith by sharing the stories of salvation proclaimed in the scriptures and relating them to their own lives and situations. Story is a way to everyone's heart and understanding; children especially become involved and enjoy stories of all types. The way in which we pass on biblical stories to children will influence the way in which they will hear the message of the scriptures proclaimed in the liturgy.

Other forms of proclamation can be used to enhance the reception of the scriptures, e.g. mime, drama, song, or choral recitation.

Responding to the word

> *All the elements that will help explain the readings should be given great consideration so that the children may make the biblical readings their own and may come more and more to appreciate the value of God's word.* (DMC 47)

Leaders will need to prepare carefully what they will say, perhaps drawing on one of the many resources available. In time they will become confident in their own reflections and in the response of the children.

The introductory comments to the scriptures and the reflection that follows the proclamation are the most important and maybe the most daunting aspect of the leader's ministry.

In a liturgy of the word with children, the reflection serves the same function as does the homily described above. In the context of the season or feast, the concerns of the gospel writer can be unfolded and the point of the particular passage related to the children's lives. The scriptures are not just stories of the past but are signs of what God is doing here and now in this assembly. The reflection will probably be a dialogue between the leader and the children, and can incorporate other forms of communication such as song, story, and image.

Bear in mind too that, in the Mass, the liturgy of the word is not an end in itself but leads into the liturgy of the eucharist. The reflection is a pivotal point in the movement of the Mass.

Be wary of replacing the reflection with activity alone, lest others perceive this gathering as a containment exercise or Sunday school rather than an act of worship.

Intercession

Liturgy is the prayerful action of the whole assembly. Children share in the prayer at their own level, absorbing the pattern and movement of the action.

As we pray with the children they learn; they adopt pattern and structure naturally: the sign of the cross, intentions for prayer, and most of all silence are absorbed into the manner of praying.

Parents, leaders and helpers will have their own prayer-life. This will communicate their regard for prayer to the children: their silence, joy and sadness, their respect for person and place, will nurture the children's prayer and allow them to express their natural sense of awe and wonder.

Silence

Silence or stillness is another integral element of liturgy. The whole way in which liturgy is celebrated should foster reflectiveness. In addition, the dialogue between God and his people which happens through the power of the Holy Spirit requires short intervals of silence. The *Directory for Masses with Children* reminds us that children are capable of reflection. They will need some guidance so that they will learn how to recollect themselves, meditate briefly, or praise or pray to God in their hearts.

Music

Music is integral to all liturgy and it is therefore integral to a liturgy of the word with children. It expresses and highlights the liturgical action; so we use music at the important moments in our liturgy: at the gospel.

An acclamation greets the gospel, a psalm can be sung in response to the word, and other responses can help express intercession and prayer. Particular songs and acclamations can be repeated throughout a liturgical season.

Recorded music can help create a prayerful atmosphere; it can also provide a useful accompaniment.

Movement to songs can help children take to heart their message and the words. Simple actions can be easily created.

There are many opportunities for music and singing within the liturgy but it is not necessary to sing everything. It is better to sing a few items well, focusing on the key points of the liturgy.

Environment

The *Directory for Masses with Children* speaks of a separate, but not too distant room (DMC 17). The place should be appropriate for liturgy: comfortable and bright, near enough to the main assembly so that valuable time is not taken up by overlong processions; far enough away so that each group can celebrate without impinging on the others' worship.

Arranging the worship space is a ministry. The space should be well prepared before the children arrive.

A focal point for the liturgy is essential, in this case a place for the proclamation of God's word rather than an altar, a place of honour for the lectionary or other book of the scriptures. A candle may be lit and colour or decoration should be used appropriate to the liturgical season or festival. Images and symbols can attract and focus the children's attention; they can be used to reflect the themes of the scriptures, the season or the feast.

Avoid arranging the worship space like a classroom with children in rows etc. Experience indicates that this is not ideal for this kind of celebration.

Ministries

Any liturgy is the action of the whole assembly, so celebrations with children also involve the adults who are present. Within the assembly, and to serve the community's worship, some people have specific roles and ministries. They should be chosen for their ability, competence, and example, since children learn through imitation. How ministers act will both enhance the celebration and show the Christian ideal of service. All involved in ministry will need to meet regularly to prepare, and to evaluate both the liturgy and their own ministry.

Leader

The leader's ministry is to open the hearts of the children to the word of God and allow them to respond to God's word in prayer and life.

The leader:

- presides over the celebration,
- welcomes the children,
- may proclaim the Gospel,
- leads the reflection on the scriptures,
- introduces and concludes the intercessions,
- facilitates the smooth running of the liturgy.

Reader

The word of God must be proclaimed audibly, clearly, reverently, with faith and understanding. The lectionary for Mass recommends that each reading be proclaimed by a different reader.

A reader:

- proclaims the scriptures,
- understands what he/she is reading,
- communicates well,
- is aware that God speaks to his people in this proclamation.

Musician

The musician:

- leads the children in song,
- enables them to pray through song,
- encourages able musicians among the children to share in this ministry.

It is not always easy to find someone to lead the music. If none of the adults have the confidence to begin a song or acclamation, the children themselves may be capable of starting. It is easier to include music in liturgies of the word with children if some of the items are used regularly and so become well known.

Priest celebrant

The priest celebrant presides over the entire liturgy of the Mass, he is a sign of the union of all the baptised in the one body of Christ. So that the separate liturgy of the word with children is seen as part of the one celebration it is important for the priest celebrant to:

- recognise the children as members of the assembly in the introduction,
- send the children and leaders with dignity to their liturgy of the word.

It can also be useful for the priest celebrant to speak to the children during the liturgy of the eucharist, for instance before the eucharistic prayer begins and at the concluding rite.

The support and encouragement of the priest to the children and to the whole worshipping community can foster a sense of ministry among the leaders.

Celebrating liturgies of the word with children

A model

1 Children gather with their families in church for the introductory rites of the Mass. After the opening song and the greeting the children, together with their leaders, are called forward.
2 A book of the scriptures is presented to a child or leader.
3 All process to a nearby place. (In some places this happens after the opening prayer.)
4 When the children have gathered the leader introduces the scripture of the day.
5 Before the gospel is proclaimed an acclamation is sung.
6 The scriptures are explored through reflection discussion and other appropriate activity.
7 There is a time of intercession for the Church, the world, those in need and the local community.
8 All return to the main body of the church for the liturgy of the eucharist.

Commentary

1 To emphasise the unity of the whole assembly the children gather in the church with their families for the introductory rites of the Mass.

2 The book of the scriptures can be presented in these or similar words:

> *Receive this book of readings*
> *and proclaim God's word faithfully*
> *to the children entrusted to your care.*

or

> *My dear children,*
> *you will now go to hear God's word,*
> *to praise God in song,*
> *and to reflect on the wonderful things*
> *God has done for us.*
> *We will await your return*
> *so that together we may celebrate the eucharist.*

3 Processions are integral to our ritual, and so the children are led by the Book which may be accompanied with candles, singing or music. Depending on the space and leaders available, the children may divide into age groups. To sustain the children's attitude of prayer the gathering action may need to be continued; this can be done through sign and gesture, song or a prayer. (There is no need for a second sign of the cross and greeting.)

4 The focus of the liturgy of the word is the proclamation of scripture. The gospel is always proclaimed but the other riches of scripture found in the Old and New Testaments should be introduced to children when appropriate. The readings are

proclaimed in ways appropriate to their content and the age of the hearers. A brief introduction may be helpful.

5 The gospel is greeted in song with alleluias or, in Lent, with another appropriate acclamation. This is the musical priority of the whole liturgy of the word.

6 There should be time after the gospel for reflection and discussion of the reading(s). This should involve the children's own experience. The reflection does not have to be limited to words alone; silence, song, drama or other activity can all help the children understand the message of the scriptures and applying it to their lives and experience.

7 All liturgy is prayer and it is right that a liturgy of the word with children should end with a time of intercession. The prayer may arise from the children's reflection but it is always concerned with the needs of the whole Church and the world. It is important to remember that the petitions are invitations to pray not the prayers themselves, so a short phrase that invites the children to pray is better than a long or detailed list of concerns. This model of intercession is easily learned by children.

Examples

Introduction

The prayer of the general intercessions is made to the Father through Christ, in the power of the Holy Spirit. Our introductions can help express this.

A *We know that God loves us,*
   so let us pray for ourselves and for others.

B *We are God's family, filled with the Holy Spirit,*
   together let us pray.

C *Jesus has told us to ask God for what we need,*
   so as God's children we pray.

Intentions

It is sufficient to state the intention, pray in the silence and respond together, for instance: *Lord, in your mercy; hear our prayer*

For all God's family
so that we may share the Good News with everyone.

For God's beautiful world
that we look after it with loving care.

For all who are hungry or sad, lonely or sick,
today we pray for . . .

For the people who live in our road
and come to our church.

Concluding prayer

The concluding prayer is a general expression of trust in God's goodness. It should be short and simple, be addressed to God (the Father) and be made through Jesus Christ our Lord.

A *Loving God,*
    we ask you to listen to these prayers
    which we bring to you today
    in the name of Jesus the Lord.
    Amen.

B *Father,*
    may your love be with us always
    and bring peace and joy to our families.
    We ask this through Jesus Christ our Lord.
    Amen.

C *God of tender love,*
   you always hear our prayers
   we ask you to grant us what we need
   through Jesus Christ our Lord.
   Amen.

8 A system is necessary to inform the group when to return to the church. An usher signalling that the homily is finished should give enough time for everything to be drawn together. The children and leaders rejoin the whole assembly for the liturgy of the eucharist.

Preparation

Preparation is essential to good liturgy. Individual liturgies should grow from reflection on the scripture of the day, how it relates to the faith experience of the people involved, and how best the gospel can be shared with the children.

The seasons of Advent, Christmas, Lent and Easter have their own rhythm. Each Sunday should be planned as part of the whole season. The scripture readings of the Sundays of Ordinary Time also have a pattern which, with forward planning, helps the preparation of individual liturgies.

Forward planning over a season also means that those Sundays and festivals can be identified when it may be more appropriate for the whole assembly to celebrate the liturgy of the word together. The great feasts of the Church's year, Christmas, Easter etc. are times for adults and children to stay together. It is a challenge to prepare liturgies that involve all the baptised.

A planning group for liturgies of the word with children involves all who have a ministry.

Together,

- they will be able to reflect on and evaluate liturgies already celebrated,

- to prepare through prayer and discussion future liturgies and co-ordinate the various tasks.

A good planning group will:

- help with the ongoing formation of its members,
- provide the opportunity to encourage potential leaders,
- and nurture the faith development of all.

Conclusion

The *Directory for Masses with Children* speaks of aims and benefits of liturgy with children in this way:

> *Various kinds of celebration may also play a major role in the liturgical formation of children and in their preparation for the Church's liturgical life. By the very fact of such celebrations children easily come to appreciate some liturgical elements, for example, greetings, silence, and common praise (especially when it is sung together). But care must be taken that the instructive element does not become dominant in these celebrations.*
>
> *Depending on the capacity of the children, the word of God should have a greater and greater place in these celebrations . . . [This] will help greatly to develop in the children an appreciation of the word of God.*
>
> *While all that has been said remains true, the final purpose of all liturgical and eucharistic formation must be a greater and greater conformity to the Gospel in the daily life of the children.* (DMC 13–15)

Appendix: Directory for Masses with Children (a summary)

Issued by the Congregation for Divine Worship, 1 November 1973. See Documents on the Liturgy 1963–1979: Conciliar, Papal and Curial Texts, *p. 676: 2134–88. Edited by ICEL. Collegeville MN: Liturgical Press, 1982. Reprinted in* The Liturgy Documents: A Parish Resource. *Edited by Elizabeth Hoffman. Chicago IL: Liturgy Training Publications, 1991. (Distributed in UK by McCrimmons).*

Sigla used

SC *Vatican Council II, Constitution on the Sacred Liturgy* Sacrosanctum Concilium, *4 December 1963. In Documents on the Liturgy, p. 1.*

GIRM *Congregation for Divine Worship,* General Instruction of the Roman Missal, *4th edition, 27 March 1975. In Documents on the Liturgy, p. 465.*

It is spiritually harmful if children 'repeatedly experience in the Church things that are barely comprehensible' (2). The purpose of the Directory is to help children:

- benefit more from the educational value of the liturgy (2)
- play a fuller part in the liturgy (3), and so be able to
- take part with more understanding in the parish Mass (21).

The liturgy must be adapted (3, 20; SC 38). The Directory gives principles for adapting to those who have not yet reached 'pre-adolescence' (6). Further adaptation applying these principles is necessary for children with special needs (6).

I The introduction of children to the eucharistic celebration

Liturgical formation (8), appropriate to their age (12); Liturgies especially for children (13), and not always Mass (see 27):

- prayer
- services of the word (see also 14).

II *Masses with adults in which children also participate*

One liturgy for the whole community is most important (16). Infants may be cared for outside of the act of worship (16). Within the liturgy, account should be taken of children:

- occasional words addressed to them: e.g. beginning and end of Mass (17); in the homily (17, 19),
- involvement of children in the action: e.g. procession with the gifts (19); singing (19),
- special liturgy of the word (17).

Sometimes, where there is a larger proportion of children:

- the homily may be addressed more directly to them,
- one of the adaptations given in chapter 3, below, may be used.

III *Masses with children in which only a few adults participate*

Recommended especially on weekdays (20).
  Further adaptation is necessary (20), in keeping with the purpose of the various elements of the liturgy outlined in the Missal (21).

- Every effort should . . . be made to increase . . . participation and to make it more intense. (22)
- The liturgy should never appear as something dry and merely intellectual. (35)

Thorough preparation by everyone is essential (29).

Involving the children

- arranging the room (22),
- visual aids (35), their own artwork (36),
- music and song (22, 30): especially the eucharistic acclamations (30); use of recorded music (32),
- reading scripture and the intercessions (22),
- dialogue with the children, especially in the homily (22, 47),
- opportunity to give reasons for thanksgivings at the start of the eucharistic prayer (22),
- silence (22, 37),
- gesture (33) and movement, especially the four processions (34): entrance, gospel, gifts, communion,
- involvement in preparing the gifts (22).

Responsibility of the priest

To make the celebration 'festive, familial and meditative' (23):

- personal preparation (23),
- manner of acting and speaking (23): especially the eucharistic prayer (52),
- actions and gestures: 'dignity, clarity, simplicity' (23).

Place and time of celebration

The criterion is to facilitate:

- 'a living liturgy that is suited to their age' (25),
- optimum receptivity (26), therefore:
- the Mass may be held in a church, or elsewhere,
- the numbers of children should not be too large (28).

Texts of the Mass

- any prayers from the Roman Missal (Sacramentary) in keeping with the season (50),
- these may be adapted, but keeping the structure and style of presidential prayers (51),
- the Apostles' Creed may be used (39),
- the Sanctus, Agnus Dei, etc. may be adapted for singing (44): *Note*: this applies only for Masses with children,
- congregational responses, the Lord's Prayer, and the trinitarian blessing formula are not to be adapted (39).

Introductory rites

One element (e.g. the greeting) plus the opening prayer are required (40); others are optional, but the elements omitted should vary.

Liturgy of the word

Scripture is obligatory (41); the gospel is always included (45).

Criterion for the decision: the spiritual value of the text for the children (44):

- the number of readings may be reduced (42),
- other texts may be chosen, in keeping with the feast or season (43),
- the text may be edited (43): simplification is often necessary, but paraphrases should be avoided (45),
- an introduction to the reading is important (47, GIRM II).

A psalm, or psalm-type hymn, or gospel acclamation (Alleluia), or silence (46).

Importance of the homily (48) and of involving the children in it (22): it may be given by one of the adults (24).

Communion rite

The Lord's Prayer, fraction, and invitation to communion are obligatory (53): 'Deliver us, Lord', 'Lord Jesus Christ' may be omitted.

Communion in both kinds: a diocese may have norms, but the cup should not be refused simply because of age.

Silent reflection is important (37).

Before the blessing, the priest should say a few words to help link the liturgy with the life of faith and with Christian witness (54).

Glossary

Ambo Also known as the lectern, it is the place from which the word of God is proclaimed during the liturgy. In the *Catechism of the Catholic Church* (1184) it is stated that 'the dignity of the word of God requires the church to have a suitable place for announcing his message so that the attention of the people may be easily directed to that place during the liturgy of the word.'

Catechetics Encompasses the theory of the religious education of children and young people, especially. This leads to catechesis, which is the practical application, including formation (see *liturgical formation*) for prayer and worship, moral formation and growth into the life and mission of the Church.

Chasuble The priest's outer vestment, worn for the celebration of Mass. It looks rather like a poncho and the colour worn relates to the liturgical season or feast day.

Chalice The cup, usually fashioned from silver or gold, used during Mass to hold the wine, which becomes the blood of Christ by the action of the Holy Spirit.

Ciborium Vessel, usually made from silver or gold, used during Mass to hold the altar breads, which become the body of Christ by the action of the Holy Spirit. Some, shaped like a shallow bowl, are called ciborium dishes; others look more like chalices with a lid. The latter are mainly used to hold the consecrated hosts kept in the tabernacle for our veneration and for distribution of Holy Communion to the sick and housebound.

Lectionary A book or list of readings of scripture for the Church's year. The Roman Catholic lectionary produced by Vatican II provides readings for every Sunday for a three-year period. Year A uses principally Matthew's Gospel, Year B, Mark's and Year C, Luke's. John's Gospel is used during the Easter season and special feasts, with chapter 6 being used during Year B. Volume ll of the lectionary contains the readings for weekday Masses and feasts, while Volume lll has selections of readings for the celebration of the sacraments, Masses for various occasions and Masses for the dead.

Liturgical formation The process that, as a result of education and experience, leads each individual towards full, conscious and active participation in the prayer life and sacramental worship of the Church. Vatican II identified liturgical formation as the proper preparation of those responsible for the teaching and celebration of the liturgy. This encompasses training in the application of liturgical principles to liturgy planning and training in the various liturgical ministries, including reader and liturgy leader.

Liturgy The public prayer and worship of the Church. The 'Constitution on the Liturgy' of Vatican II describes the liturgy as 'the summit towards which the activity of the Church is directed; at the same time it is the fountain from which all her power flows' (10).

Novena Nine-day preparation for a particular Solemnity, such as Pentecost, which is marked by special prayers each day.

Ordo Liturgical calendar published each year by every diocese, listing the Sundays, Solemnities, Holy Days of Obligation as well as feast days proper to that diocese or country. It also includes the cycle of prayer, giving intentions for prayer on particular dates or during particular seasons.

Penitential Service Communal celebration comprising a liturgy of the word and, usually, a liturgical action, such as placing a stone or an autumn leaf at the foot of the cross to symbolize our desire to let

go of the burden of sinfulness and seek to be renewed in our disciple-
ship of the Lord.

Penitential Services do not include the individual confession of sin,
absolution or penance and so this liturgy may be celebrated in the
absence of a priest.

Penitential Services are of value in helping form our consciences,
developing greater awareness of personal and social sin and prompt-
ing action for social justice and peace. They are particularly valuable
as a preparation for the eventual celebration of the Sacrament of
Reconciliation for children and for adults preparing for baptism.

Presider This role is one of service – animating and encouraging
the gifts and ministries of the assembly so that the Church may be
built up in its life of holiness, its ministries and its mission to
herald the reign of God. The priest is the presider for the celebration
of the Eucharist, acting as the representative of Christ and the
Church.

Lay people may be trained (and commissioned) to preside during a
liturgy other than the Mass. Thus, they may be presiders for a liturgy
of the word. Some parishes are already accustomed to lay presiders
during celebrations of the word and Communion in the absence of a
priest.

The fundamental reason for every liturgical celebration needing
someone to preside is that no celebrating assembly can exist except
in the name of Christ and called together by Christ, rooted in the
living tradition of the catholic and apostolic faith. This reality is
what presidency in the assembly expresses.

Reconciliation Liturgy A communal celebration of the Sacrament of
Reconciliation. It is comprised of a liturgy of the word with the
opportunity for individual confession and absolution. Some celebrations of Rite ll, as it is called, leave the impression that the liturgy of
the word is merely a preparation for the sacrament, which is then
celebrated with individual confession and individual absolution.
Such experiences reinforce the view that Rite ll is 'inadequately communal and insufficiently personal'. The communal dimension may be

weak if a sense of community does not already exist and if there is no interaction, except possibly sharing the sign of peace.

The major practical problem with Rite ll is that of being able to recruit sufficient confessors so that priests and people have adequate time for individual confession without lengthening that part of the liturgy unduly. In practice, the ratio of priests to penitents is usually inadequate. This can constrain priests and penitents alike to minimize the confessional encounter, penitents perhaps being asked to name only the main area of their sinfulness and those in urgent need of spiritual counsel being asked to seek out the confessor again after the liturgy. Nevertheless, the support of communal prayer, the example of the community and the brevity of the form of confession can be particularly helpful for people seeking to be reconciled after many years' absence from the sacraments. However, the decreasing number of priests will inevitably restrict the use of Rite ll to groups of a manageable size.

Resources

Liturgical books

Children's lectionary

There are a few versions available, approved as resource books for use in England and Wales. *Lectionary for Masses with Children*, published by Liturgical Training Publications (1993), comes in four volumes, in hardback – one for each year of the three-year liturgical cycle and one for weekdays and feasts. It is also published in paperback as a study edition. Although it is cheaper than hardback, it is less durable and does not look as dignified. However, cost will be a consideration if the parish has two or three age groups of children, each group going to their own liturgy room and needing their own children's lectionary! There are beautiful hardback editions that contain the three-year cycle, the weekdays and feasts, all in one. The one disadvantage is that they are rather heavy for a young child to carry.

Eucharistic Prayers for Masses with Children and Masses of Reconciliation, published by McCrimmon (1975).

Reference

See the 'Diocesan Ordo' in the *Diocesan Directory* for a calendar of the year so as to check the Sunday of the year or Solemnity to be celebrated. It is usually on sale in parishes and diocesan bookshops.

Child Protection Guidelines, available from your diocesan child protection office.

Additional resource books

In the list below I have included resource books that I have used or know about. The list is not exhaustive – there are other resource books available – but serves as a useful pointer to liturgically correct sources of help.

Gather the Children by Mary Catherine Berglund, published by the Pastoral Press (1987–95). There are three volumes, one for each year of the liturgical cycle. The appearance of the text can be rather off-putting at first, but disregard this, for this is the resource book I have found most valuable and recommend most highly of all the ones I have used. It offers ideas for separate liturgies of the word for children of several age ranges, as well as some examples of penitential rites and simplified creeds.

Sunday–Weekly Leader Guide by Christiane Brusselmans, Sister Paule Freeburg DC, Reverend Edward Matthews and Christopher Walker, published by T. Shand Publications (1990–92) and available from ViewPoint Resources Direct. The text includes a first reading as well as the Gospel for every Sunday, Feast Day and Solemnity, and a simple psalm setting and Gospel acclamation, which would be particularly valuable for an instrumentalist or singer.

A Good Friday Liturgy for Young Children by Barbara Mary Hopper, published by McCrimmon (1997).

Celebrating Advent and Christmas Liturgies with Young Children by Barbara Mary Hopper, published by McCrimmon (1998).

Note: In the descriptions of the following publications, I have highlighted what I think may be helpful, but it is important to use these resources selectively, keeping in mind the essential elements of the liturgy.

The Complete Children's Liturgy Book by Katie Thompson, published by Kevin Mayhew (1997), is a one-volume book covering the three-year cycle with photocopyable pages. The 'discussion' sections are good, but you would need to have Intercessions, not a 'closing prayer'.

Welcome! by Jenny Pate, published by HarperCollins (1989), covers the three-year cycle in one book. Written to help with celebrations for young children, it has some good questions to help set the scene for the Gospel reading. A completely revised edition has been published by McCrimmon (2003).

Welcome the Word by Joan Brown SND, in a new edition published by Geoffrey Chapman (1996), consists of two volumes covering the three-year cycle. This edition includes notes on each liturgical season and Gospel passage for the liturgy leaders, to help deepen their understanding and faith. Photocopyable worksheets are available in a separate volume.

Recommended reading

A Child Shall Lead Them by Gerard A. Pottebaum, Sister Paule Freeburg DC, and Joyce M. Kelleher, published by Treehaus Communications, Inc. (1992). A guide to celebrating the word with children. Available from ViewPoint Resources Direct from its website at www.viewpoint24.com

Children in the Assembly of the Church, edited by Eleanor Bernstein and John Brooks-Leonard, published by Liturgy Training Publications (1993). In it, five authors look at various aspects of celebrating liturgy with children.

The Spirit of the Child by David Hay with Rebecca Nye, published by HarperCollins*Religious* (1998). A thorough and revealing examination of the spiritual potential of children. Available from ViewPoint Resources Direct (see details of website above).

To Walk with a Child by Gerard A. Pottebaum, published by Treehaus Communications, Inc. (1993). This book, subtitled, *A Guide to Homiletics for Children,* is also available from ViewPoint Resources Direct.

Visual aids

'Quadri Biblici' – an excellent series of 80 posters covering Old and New Testament readings – published by Editrice Elledici, Leumann, Turin, Italy, and available from Pauline Books & Media, 199 Kensington High Street, London W8 6BA, telephone 020 7937 9591.

Clip Art for the Liturgical Year (1988) by Clemens Schmidt (illustrator) and Joshua J. Jeide (ed.), The Liturgical Press, Minnesota.

- Slides and slide projector. A plain wall can be used instead of a screen. Occasionally, the use of one or two appropriate slides can be very helpful to introduce the theme or as part of the dialogue. The images need to be projected at the eye level of the children.
- A candle in a candle holder.
- A crucifix, ideally one on a stand.
- A low table, such as a coffee table, with a cloth or even a set of cloths in the liturgical colours of green, red, purple, white or gold.
- Pictures from out-of-date calendars. Each New Year, a request could be made in the parish newsletter for old calendars with pictures of people, scenery, animals and so on suitable for use as visual aids for the children's liturgy.
- A fabric-covered freestanding display board suitable for use with pieces of Velcro.

Music

Hymns Old and New with Supplement (1989), Kevin Mayhew (ed.), with Tony Barr and Robert Kelly, Kevin Mayhew, Bury St Edmunds.

The following music resources are obtainable from ViewPoint Resources Direct (*website:* www.viewpoint24.com) or Decani Music (*website:* www.decanimusic.co.uk). Other useful websites are www.giamusic.com and www.ocp.org.

Only songbooks and CDs are mentioned here, but many of the songbooks actually include additional instrumental parts, photocopyable 'assembly editions' and guidance notes, while the CDs often include karaoke-style backing tracks for rehearsal (or when instrumentalists are not available). Some resources have additional formats, such as cassettes, choreography books, instrument packs and much more. It is certainly worth asking your distributor what is available.

Behold the Lamb by Mark Friedman, Janet Vogt and Donna Anderle, published by OCP Publications. This contains music and readings for young people for Lent and Easter. A two-CD set is also available.

Calling the Children by Christopher Walker, published by OCP Publications. A two-CD set is also available.

Children at Heart by Paul Inwood, published by OCP Publications. A CD is also available.

Enter the Journey by Mark Friedman and Janet Vogt, published by OCP Publications. A two-CD set is also available.

Jubilee Mass by Owen Alstott, published by OCP Publications.

Laudate (1999) Stephen Dean (ed.), Decani Music, Mildenhall, Suffolk.

Litany of the Word (Advent Litany) by Bernadette Farrell, published by OCP Publications.

Music for Children's Liturgy of the Word by Christopher Walker, published by OCP Publications, consisting of a book for each year of the three-year cycle and a two-CD set to match each book.

Share the Light by Bernadette Farrell, published by OCP Publications. Nine of the fourteen songs are supported by sign language (American and British) illustrations. CD and CD-ROM sets are available, including performances of the songs, instrumental backing tracks and video of the songs performed using signed support.

When Children Gather, compiled by Robert W. Piercy and Vivian E. Williams, published by GIA Publications, Inc. A two-CD set is also available.

References and further reading

'Constitution on the Liturgy' in *Documents of Vatican II*, Walter M. Abbott and Joseph Gallagher (eds), G. Chapman, London, pp. 137–78.

Dean, S. (1994) 'A Word for Children', *Priests & People*, vol. 8, no. 6, pp. 232–5.

Gaupin, L. (1992) 'Separate Liturgies of the Word with Children?' in *Children in the Assembly of the Church*, Eleanor Bernstein and John Brooks-Leonard (eds), Liturgy Training Publications, Chicago, pp. 65–80.

McNaspy, C.J. (1966) 'Liturgy' in *Documents of Vatican II*, Walter M. Abbott and Joseph Gallagher (eds), G. Chapman, London, pp. 133–6.

Nelson, G. Mueller (1992) 'Adults and Children in the Art of Celebration' in *Children in the Assembly of the Church*, Eleanor Bernstein and John Brooks-Leonard (eds), Liturgy Training Publications, Chicago, pp. 51–64.

O'Brien, John. J. (1990) 'Eucharist and Children' in *The New Dictionary of Sacramental Worship*, Peter E. Fink (ed.), The Liturgical Press, Minnesota, pp. 184–7.

Philibert, P. (1987) 'Readiness for Ritual: Psychological Aspects of Maturity' in 'Christian Celebration' in *Alternative Futures for Worship*, Bernard J. Lee (general ed.), vol. 1, The Liturgical Press, Minnesota.

Rummery, G. and Lundy, D. (1982) *Growing into Faith*, Darton, Longman & Todd, London.

Searle, M. (1992) 'Children in the Assembly of the Church' in *Children in the Assembly of the Church*, Eleanor Bernstein and

John Brooks-Leonard (eds), Liturgy Training Publications, Chicago, pp. 30–50.

Vos, J. Patano (1992) 'Unpacking the Directory for Masses with Children' in *Children in the Assembly of the Church*, Eleanor Bernstein and John Brooks-Leonard (eds), Liturgy Training Publications, Chicago, pp. 81–99.

Wilde, James A. (1990) 'Liturgies for Children' in *The New Dictionary of Sacramental Worship*, Peter E. Fink (ed.), The Liturgical Press, Minnesota, pp. 191–9.

My children's liturgy address book

Diocesan contacts

Name: ....

Tel: ....

e-mail: ....

Name: ....

Tel: ....

e-mail: ....

Parish details

Tel: ....

e-mail: ....

Children's liturgy leader

Name: ....

Tel: ....

e-mail: ....

Members of children's liturgy team

Name:...

Tel: ....

e-mail: ....

Name:...

Tel: ....

e-mail: ....

Name:...

Tel: ....

e-mail: ....

Name:...

Tel: ....

e-mail: ....

Name:...

Tel: ....

e-mail: ....

Rota organizer

Name:...

Tel: ....

e-mail: ....